COLLEGE
KNOWLEDGE

101 Tips

D1310624

DAVID SCHOEM

THE UNIVERSITY OF MICHIGAN PRESS
Ann Arbor

Copyright © by the University of Michigan 2005
All rights reserved
Published in the United States of America by
The University of Michigan Press
Manufactured in the United States of America
♾ Printed on acid-free paper

2016   2015   2014   2013   10   9   8   7

A CIP catalog record for this book is available from the British Library.

Library of Congress Cataloging-in-Publication Data

Schoem, David Louis.
    College knowledge : 101 tips for the college-bound student / David
Schoem.
       p.   cm.
    ISBN 0-472-03035-3 (pbk. : alk. paper)
    1. College student orientation—United States.   I. Title.

    LB2343.3.S343   2005
    378.1'98—dc22   2004029698

ISBN 978-0-472-03035-4 (pbk. : alk. paper)

COLLEGE KNOWLEDGE

"Professor Schoem has a breadth of knowledge on the intricacies of University life that is unparalleled."

—Jeff Nelson, former Schoem student,
Teach for America, Chicago

"David Schoem has always been a committed advocate for students. He translates the best research and practices into suggestions that students can use as a tool kit for their social and emotional growth. His comprehensive coverage of topics and real world experiences can reach students from varied backgrounds."

—James A. Anderson, Vice President for
Student Success, SUNY, Albany

"What a find for any college student! In no one other place can you find information with this much depth about the all important transition between high school and college."

—Erica Greenstein, former Schoem student

"David Schoem's book is a much needed resource for students and faculty alike. It is a handbook for student success for everyone."

—Judith Patton, Director, University Studies,
Portland State University

"The sound advice in this book will help ease the transition to college for students—it comes directly from those who have survived the experience and have thrived."

—Sylvia Hurtado, Director, Higher Education
Research Institute, UCLA

"Schoem's practical tips spring from his wisdom. . . . This book speaks not only to prospective and first-year college students but also to us, their families."

—Stephen H. Sumida, Professor of American Ethnic Studies,
University of Washington

"In an overcrowded market regarding advice for college students, the wisdom, common sense and good humor of this book stand out. Ignore it at your own risk."

—Harold Shapiro, Former President, Princeton University;
Former President, University of Michigan

To My Students

Preface

The first year of college is an exhilarating experience. It is a year when the rush of adrenaline alone is enough to carry a student forward on most days. Time moves in the extreme, as the excitement of much greater freedom and independence, stimulating courses, and new friends makes everything speed by.

It is critical that students come to college intellectually and emotionally prepared for the academic and social experience that awaits them. College is a qualitatively different experience than high school, and students' expectations need to be set appropriately. The transition from high school to college is so significant that it can be difficult for most without some preparation. The most successful college students I have known have modeled the advice that follows in this book.

I encourage students reading this book who will be entering college or who are already in their first year of college to carry these ideas with you to help insure that your transition goes well. Read the tips, digest them, and keep them close by for the many moments when you may need some direction and support. Then brace yourself for the ride of a lifetime—the first year of college.

Every tip and vignette in this book has for me brought up memories of the many wonderful students I have taught and counseled throughout my career. Each tip and vignette reflects a composite of enlightening experiences and conversations with multiple students with whom I have worked. It has made the writing of this book very special in a way that is quite different from other books I have authored and edited.

I feel so fortunate, particularly as a first-generation college student, to have pursued a profession and an avocation that have enabled me to study social scientific theory about K–12 and higher education; intergroup relations across race, ethnicity, and religion; social stratification; civic engagement and community life; and social change. All the while, I have had the opportunity to put theory into practice, working directly with thousands of intellectually creative, dynamic, and caring students.

In recent years I have become increasingly committed to efforts to bring intellectual scholarship to the public domain. Too often, what we know, publish, discuss, and reward in the academy never leaves our small world. I applaud the University of Michigan Press for adopting this book and hope that it will inspire more of my colleagues in higher education to reach out to the public. This book, while clearly written for a more popular audience, is still rooted in substantive academic scholarship and extensive practice in the field.

I have been in one or another teaching role since I was about fifteen years old. Along this journey, I have been a day-care, nursery school, and elementary school teacher's assistant at alternative and traditional schools both here in the United States and in the British Infant Schools. I have taught and tutored secondary school students, and I received a secondary school teaching certificate in Massachusetts. I taught military officers for college credit at Alameda Naval Base and taught basic English and math skills at a business school in Richmond, California. I have taught graduate students and served on dissertation committees. I have led numerous seminars, consultations, and workshops for faculty from small and large, private and public, urban and rural, regional and elite colleges and universities. I have been very active in national organizations devoted to higher education and the improvement of undergraduate education.

I have spent most of my career working in the area of undergraduate education. Subsequent to my own education at the University of Michigan, Harvard University, and the University of California at Berkeley, I have been a professor, dean, and vice president for academic affairs and student affairs. In those various roles, I have been involved in almost all aspects of undergraduate education at one time or another, from curriculum committees to diversity and undergraduate initiatives to advisory boards on student life. I have both written about and developed initiatives on learning communities, first-year seminars, and intergroup dialogues, among many other topics. I have written extensively about many aspects of higher education and worked closely with inspiring colleagues across the nation who have dedicated their lives to improving undergraduate education in the United States.

Much of my time, commitment, and effort, however, have gone to working directly with undergraduate students, as their teacher, advisor, program director, mentor, and friend. I have benefited enormously from my relationships with my students, growing and learning from each outstanding individual I have met. I hope this book in some small way expresses my gratitude for all that they have given to me.

Acknowledgments

This book has been many years in the making. In addition to teaching and counseling individual students throughout my career, about ten years ago I began to get requests to provide tips for college success to incoming students at summer and fall orientations. Faculty and college administrators from different campuses would call me for advice for their children and grandchildren who were about to enter college as undergraduates. Later, my friends started sending their children to college and would approach me with questions.

Given these experiences, the tips for this book have come quickly and easily. As I've written the book, I have received many suggestions from friends, parents, and respected colleagues. Lynn Adelman and Anna and Joshua Gotlieb offered good suggestions at the start as did Rosa Maria Cabello, George Cooper, Debra Humphreys, and Wendy Woods later on. Yitze Miller, Josh Wall, and Allen Weinstock offered their encouragement, support, and most importantly, their lifelong friendship. Nancy Thomas, as always, provided ideas, perspective, and support that were invaluable throughout the process.

I have relied on my students as the best source for verification and confirmation of the ideas in this book. However, I do take full responsibility for its contents. The very bright students in my Sociology 105 class, Democracy, Diversity, and Community, were highly enthusiastic in their feedback and support, as were Leah Beasley and the talented students in my Sociology 458 class, Sociology of Education. Tori Greene, one of our nation's future outstanding teachers and educational leaders, was at the ready to provide concrete help when asked. Sara Firestone was a great help in doing research when I first started developing this book. Julie Butchart provided enormously useful feedback on several of the chapters. I am most indebted to Alexa Phillips. I met Alexa during her first semester at college, when she was an outstanding student in my first-year seminar course. In her senior year she offered to help with this book, providing critical suggestions, insights, and feedback on the tips and vignettes. Alexa is a very talented writer and thinker and I look forward to reading her first book in the years ahead.

I am most fortunate to be completing my third book with the wonderful editors and staff of the University of Michigan Press. Mary Erwin has been my editor and champion for this book as well as for *Inside Separate Worlds: Life Stories of Young Blacks, Jews, and Latinos* and *Intergroup Dialogue: Deliberative Democracy in School, College, Community, and Workplace.* Mary is supportive, imaginative, and highly talented as an editor and administrator. I also thank Christina Milton, who has provided outstanding copyediting for each of my books as managing editor of the press. Thanks also go to Philip Pochoda, director of the press; Mike Kehoe, director of sales; Peter Sickman-Garner, director of marketing, and Mary Bisbee-Beek, publicist. All have been as helpful as possible.

Finally, I wish to thank my loving family for bearing with me through yet another intensive writing experience on this, my seventh book. Karyn, Adina, and Shana gave constant encouragement and offered lots of humor, constantly joking and asking for news about the latest tip. A recent homemade Father's Day card declared, "Tip #101: A family who loves you with all of their hearts!" Karyn's support and love have been steadfast, and Adina and Shana, now college students, have made me want even more to get the book in print quickly to catalog for them all the advice I have offered to other students over the years. They are outstanding students and independent young adults whom I love, respect, and admire tremendously. These days I increasingly find myself listening intently to their ideas and advice in place of offering my own. I guess that's Tip #102: Listen to your children.

Contents

Getting the Most out of College

Faculty and Classes

Expanding Your Social Boundaries

Campus Life

Health and Safety

Family, Finances, and the Details of Daily Life

The Top 10 Tips for College Success and Happiness

1 Believe in Yourself

I can't overstate the importance of maintaining your self-confidence at college. You are a bright, capable person, and if you have good study habits and the desire to succeed, you will do just that at each and every college that offered you admission. Know that this is true, remind yourself daily, and never question your intellectual abilities.

There is a mind game that gets played out at every college regardless of its guidebook ranking. Very simply, students worry that they're not up to the college's standard. Unfortunately, colleges do very little to allay such fears. First-year students look at their peers in the residence hall cafeteria, at the college convocation, or at the first lecture or seminar and worry that they're just not as smart as the other students.

Many students, when they are speaking openly to me, wonder aloud whether the college admissions office made a mistake in admitting them. Deep down in a vulnerable place inside them, they imagine that if the college admissions office had truly read their applications carefully, they would not have been deserving of admission. After all, with so many other smart students in their school and now sitting with them in college, how could they have been fully competitive and worthy of admission.

I experienced this same fear when I attended college many years ago. Sure, I was a good student in high school, but I worried that I would be found out once I got to college. Maybe the admissions office accidentally put my application in the wrong pile and sent me the wrong letter. I wondered whether colleges ever send out "so sorry" letters retracting admissions to students like me.

Of course this is all silliness. And if such a notion should ever come over you, just let go of it immediately. College admissions offices know what they're doing. The truth is that colleges receive applications from so many outstanding students that they must reject hundreds, even thousands, of qualified students. So, clearly, everyone who is admitted is fully capable of doing outstanding work. The key is discovering what your interests are, finding your own identity, meeting good students and faculty, and developing good study skills.

When you hear others talk about all the smart kids at college, know that they're talking about you. SAT/ACT scores? Once you're in college, no one cares about those exams and what your score was. Your high school GPA? Forget it. After the first few weeks of college, high school will seem like years in the past. No one is interested. What faculty members and the other students will be interested in is you—in your ideas, your interests, what you care about, what classes you are taking, papers you are writing, books you are reading, and what you hope to accomplish in your life.

When I first entered high school in ninth grade with a class of 1,500 other students, our principal gave a welcoming speech to us in our huge high school auditorium. He told us to look at the student sitting next to us on our right and then to turn and look at the student sitting next to us on our left. Then he told us that in four years, at the end of twelfth grade, one of the three of us would not be there for graduation. I remember that sorry speech and its negative message all too well.

But unlike my high school principal's advice, you should approach your college education with full confidence that you will graduate in four years. And your expectation should be not just that you will graduate but that you will excel. In college you will begin the path of realizing your academic, professional, and personal dreams.

Right now, take out a piece of paper and write down the following. "I know I am smart. I know I can do well in college. I believe in myself and in my academic abilities. I will achieve to the top of my ability. I will accomplish great things." Put this paper in a secret place. Read it to yourself as often as you need. Self-confidence is your first insurance policy for success in college.

2 Learn to Be a College Student: You're Not in High School Anymore

College is an entirely different universe than high school, and your job is to explore that new universe as you move on to the rest of your life. College is not just different but is also a far richer, more substantive, and deeper learning environment than high school. It's important to come to college mentally prepared and with the right expectations for your college experience. Get ready to immerse yourself in an entirely different type and quality of learning.

The worst mistake you can make is to imagine that college is like high school. That's a nightmarish vision. Think about it. Only if you had failed twelfth grade would you still be in high school. Fortunately, you were a very successful high school student, and your reward and opportunity is to go on to the great educational adventure that is college. Don't waste the next four years of your life repeating your high school experience.

At the end of four years of high school, you, along with the other best-educated students in the country, typically know five areas of intellectual thought, including math, science, English, U.S. history, and a second language. To be certain, these are important fields. But a world of ideas awaits you when you enter college.

Most colleges, in their effort to help guide you in the process of broadening your intellectual horizons, require you to take a series of required courses in various disciplinary areas. Unfortunately, too many students embrace these requirements in the old high school mold. They organize their course selection for their first year of college in a manner that will help them "get the requirements out of the way." Please, don't approach your first year of college as yet another year of ugly requirements, forcing you to delay for yet another year the excitement of learning that awaits you.

What steps can you take in your first year to embrace the best that college has to offer? First, take at least one first-year seminar. In a first-year seminar, you will sit in a class of between twelve and twenty students with a faculty member who loves to teach undergraduates, exploring with other bright students a field in which you all have an interest. Most importantly, you will build a small community of interested learners, students and faculty, meeting a few times each week to question, challenge, analyze, and think about ideas that are important to you and the world around you. The small seminar setting is the epitome of the college experience.

Second, take courses with good teachers. Regardless of how interested you are in any given course content or course description, you are better off following good teachers. With good teachers you will be inspired, you will be engaged, you will build a relationship, and you will want to do good work and to learn beyond the limits of the course syllabus.

Third, try out a new idea. It is the very essence of college. College is a place filled with people who think about ideas. This is a chance you must not miss out on, a chance to give voice to all your ideas—the wondrous ones, the ones that will some day save lives, the inventive ones, and also those that are half-baked, barely formed, and on face value seem almost ridiculous. Trying out an idea is so exciting in college because there is a community of faculty and friends who will take you seriously and listen and respond to you.

Fourth, try out a new field of study that you've never considered before. Take a course in some field in which you know very little or even nothing. Yes, there's some risk here. You might find out you're not particularly interested in this field. But if you consider how many years you've been studying the same old topic, over and over and over again without any choice, as if there were only a handful of topics in the world to study, this is a pretty small risk. And the benefits could be enormous. Take some intellectual risks, please!

Fifth, try out a new career. No, most of you don't have to start looking for full-time work just yet. But imagine what life will be like for you if you choose to be an artist, a teacher, a CEO, a writer, a scientist, an engineer, a doctor, a survey researcher, an interpreter, a community organizer, a forest ranger. Many students come to college thinking that their career

5

choices are limited to medicine, law, engineering, and business. Don't think in that limiting way; your career choices are wide open.

Sixth, try out a new friend. High school friendships can be comforting and supportive as you enter an entirely new environment, but if you want to move on with your life and meet the world, then college is precisely the time to assert yourself, make new friends, and pursue your own identity. Students in your college will come from all backgrounds—racial, ethnic, class, religious, sexual orientation, geographic, and national—and you should meet these people.

Seventh, try out a new perspective. You might change your perspective or reaffirm your current viewpoint, but in doing so you will most definitely begin to take responsibility for thinking critically and holding your own views. And, hopefully, you'll begin to see the world beyond factoids and sound bites and understand the complexities of issues. See the world from a point of view of someone who has different interests, comes from a different part of the country, or is of a different gender or race.

3   Get to Know Faculty

Getting to know faculty at your college must be one of your top priorities. It will make your college experience.

Don't consider yourself an A student if you don't know at least one professor well enough to ask a question, ask for advice, discuss some academic topic, and request a letter of recommendation. You haven't completed your college education yet. And if you know one or more faculty well and you're not an A or B student, you have greatly increased the chances that you will walk at graduation in four years alongside your peers. It is well known that students who succeed in college have good relationships with one or more faculty members.

One way to think about faculty is that they are brilliant scholars, cutting-edge researchers, inspiring teachers, first-rate authors, and consultants to leaders in every imaginable field around the globe. For most first-year students, that's a surefire intimidating mind-set that will permanently keep you fifty yards away from the nearest faculty member in sight.

I suggest you step back from that approach for a moment. Try imagining your professor as a parent, a child, a sibling. A professor is someone who likes to spend much of his or her day reading, creating, thinking, discovering, experimenting, writing, and engaging in interesting discussions with smart people just like you.

Faculty are regular people, just like you. Faculty have their good points and their flaws. They have their likes and dislikes. They worry about money, health, and taxes; watch sports; take an interest in politics; have close friends; and sometimes are in good, friendly moods but on other days are the opposite. What distinguishes faculty from others, however, is their interest in ideas as a lifelong pursuit.

This characteristic of faculty makes getting to know them such a special and unique opportunity. You get to spend four years in their environment—in their classes, their labs, their offices, their lecture halls, their campus hangouts—during which time your primary purpose is to pursue ideas and the intellectual life. It's in this sense that college is so different from high school. These faculty people don't just come to work to teach you. They live and breathe their intellectual work twenty-four hours a day, and they're delighted to have you join them in their journey during your short stay in their environment. Don't miss out!

So how do you meet a faculty member? The best approach is to meet them in the classroom by taking a small enough class or seminar that personal relationships naturally develop. You see the professor a few times a week in class, they debate ideas with you, and they read your papers and write back to you with insightful comments. You'll likely feel comfortable meeting with them after class or during office hours.

But because many of your classes won't be small seminars, it's important to take advantage of other approaches to meet faculty. Go up to the faculty member after class and follow up on a question or idea that was raised in class. Do the same during office hours. Check to see if there are any opportunities to be a research assistant for a faculty member. Some colleges have mentor programs to provide structure for meeting faculty. Invite your faculty member to eat lunch with you in your residence hall, at a student union cafeteria, or at a local sandwich shop. Ask your professor if he/she would be willing to speak at a meeting of some organization you're a part of. Join a college committee that includes students as another way to meet and talk with faculty.

And if you are fortunate enough to have a professor who invites your class over to his/her house for dinner, by all means, GO! No excuses are acceptable. Don't assume you will ever have this opportunity again in college. As one very bright student told me recently, if your faculty member invites you to *anything,* GO!

What should you say to your professors when you do decide you're ready to talk with them? Ask them about themselves, about what they do, about how they got interested in their field. Ask them what they're working on now, whether it is a new research project, a journal article, a book, a community project, a conference presentation. Tell them about a book you're reading or something you've been wondering about related to your class. Feel free to talk about any topic related directly or indirectly to the class. Tell them about your own intellectual and social interests and about your professional goals. All of these questions and topics will lead to enriching conversations and friendships that you will maintain throughout college and, in many cases, well beyond.

Finally, you will want to know a professor well enough that you can ask that person for a recommendation letter. In most cases, you will be rewarded with such kind words in the letter that you'll find yourself thrilled at how proud the academic world is of your intellectual pursuits and accomplishments.

DAN PARKER—*"Tutoring Is for A Students."*

Dan Parker is taking the pre-business curricular track. He has always known that he would be good in business, and his parents have always encouraged and assumed that this would be his career. In high school his dad set up summer internships for him in business, and Dan has loved following the stock market in the daily newspaper.

Dan started off his first semester with a course load that included calculus and economics. The first few weeks of math class were mostly review from high school, and Dan felt very confident about his academic preparation and performance. He needed only to study a couple nights a week to stay on pace with the course.

All of a sudden, or so it seemed, the course picked up steam. The material the professor began to cover was all new to Dan, and the problem sets were quite difficult. And there were so many of them! Dan was used to just studying a few hours per week on each subject, and he didn't have the study habits in place to put in sufficient time to keep up. Within two weeks time with the new material, Dan realized that he was falling way behind and his first major test was coming up the next week.

Dan had always been an A or B student. He had never received lower than a B in high school. Yet, on his first test, Dan got a C−, having missed all the questions testing the material he had not already learned in high school. Dan was embarrassed to say anything to anyone about getting help because he never had to seek help in high school. In fact, he had been a math tutor in high school. Dan began to worry that all his plans for a career in business were not going to be realized.

After the first test, Dan couldn't help but observe that many other students were upset about their grades. Although people were grousing about the professor and how she should have explained the material better, a few students mentioned that they were going to participate in study groups. They invited Dan to join them, and grudgingly he agreed.

When Dan attended his first study group session, he recognized that there were all levels of students present. He didn't think some of the students were so smart, but he also knew that others were the absolute stars of the class and had received A grades on the exam. He was surprised to see such a mix of students there. During the study session, a number of students spoke of meeting the professor during office hours to get help on certain questions. Others mentioned that they were also going to the math department's "math lab" for extra assistance.

All of this was entirely new to Dan. Yes, he had read about the math lab in the course syllabus. And, yes, he knew his teacher consistently invited students to office hours. But Dan had always thought that going for help was not for people like him. He decided to give it a try because he knew he had to do better on his exams.

Dan started taking advantage of all of these resources—office hours, math lab, and the study group. It wasn't as bad as he thought, and no one stigmatized him for asking for help. In fact, he got lots of positive feedback from his friends and parents for his effort and interest. He found that he was starting to pick up the new material and had a group of friends who shared his struggle.

Dan's confidence and determination got a big boost from all of this work, he began to put in many additional hours studying, and he again started to feel that he could achieve his goals. Next exam, Dan got a B+, and on his final he got an A−.

4 Get Involved and Be Engaged

It is highly important to your success in college that you feel attached to your college and are involved in campus life. Not only is it important for your mental and emotional well-being, but it is also a central ingredient for your academic success. Students who feel a connection to their college are much more likely to do well there, to go on to graduate, and to report having had positive college experiences.

It's probably easier at first glance to understand the importance of being involved if you are attending a large, public university. At a large university, there may be fifteen thousand, twenty thousand, thirty-five thousand, or even forty thousand or more students on campus. Coming from a high school and perhaps a neighborhood in which it seemed just about everyone knew, admired, and cared about you, you may naturally feel isolated and lonely. How will you ever stand out and be noticed as the unique and special individual that you are?

As a student who has purposely chosen a small, liberal arts college, you may anticipate that you've already addressed this concern by your selection of a small college. But in a surprising way, the small, close experience of your college can result in some feelings that are very similar to those of your peers at large public universities. After all, if you find yourself feeling lonely and homesick at a small college, it's likely that you'll attribute these feelings as being your own doing rather than the fault of the college's size or impersonal atmosphere. At your college, everyone appears to be nice and interested in each individual, and students know one another, yet you are experiencing college feeling like you're an outsider, on the periphery.

What to do? The simple answer is to get involved. And by getting involved, you may want to attempt a variety of strategies, reaching beyond just that which worked for you in high school. Especially if you are attending college with friends from high school, you should definitely explore—on your own—getting involved in campus activities, events, and organizations.

Most colleges have academic structures whose very purpose is to create smaller, more personal, learning environments. One popular structure is called "learning communities." Typically, these programs have the best teachers in the university. They may be academic programs located in the residence hall where you live, or they may be organized as two or more courses together, not associated with any housing situation.

In addition, many colleges today have programs for undergraduates to participate in research with faculty. While this may sound intimidating to a new college student, it is, in fact, one of the best ways to get to know (and be known by) faculty and students on a personal basis.

Community service learning is another organized feature on most campuses, and a growing number of campuses are now offering course-based intergroup dialogues. These courses bring students together from two or more social identity groups to talk openly and frankly about difficult issues between groups.

Then there are the myriad campus organizations. Every college has student organizations to suit your interests in politics, sports, media, art, music and theater, writing, race and ethnicity, religion, and so on.

Academic departments often have student clubs for those who would like to pursue in more depth their interest in chemistry, genetics, creative writing, language, politics, or whatever.

In addition to the option of getting involved in an organization, every day opportunities exist on campus and off to attend lectures, concerts, or plays; to participate in intramural sports or pick-up games; and to do all kinds of other things. Read the student newspaper, check the postings on campus bulletin boards and telephone poles, and find an event to get you out of your room into the residence hall and out into the campus community.

Some students will want to go beyond attending events or participating in organizations. There are numerous opportunities to become student leaders on campus in existing organizations or academic clubs, and students can even set up their own organizations. There often are workshops and retreats to gain experience and skills in leadership and all kinds of networks of student leaders.

These wonderful opportunities will allow you to feel connected intellectually and socially to college life. And be sure not to let yourself feel overwhelmed. Take things slowly, make your choices carefully, and manage your time carefully. You will have four—or more—years to try out these academic and social options, so don't rush to get all of this done in the first few weeks of college.

5   Expand Your Comfort Zone

The first days of college can be rather intimidating socially. After four or more years with the same group of friends, having established a reputation among your peers and teachers, having been a leader in school and community groups, and having been recognized as a very special person, you now have to start all over. Or so it seems at the time. At this anxious moment, many students are inclined to withdraw to what feels most comfortable, which is their homogeneous, high school friendship circle.

High school friends are good and fine, but it's a mistake to retreat to them just for security. It's a mistake because now you are in college and you don't have to repeat your high school experience. In college you should be experiencing new friends, new ideas, new worlds.

College truly is the time for you to meet the world from which you've been secluded for most of your life. It's like being sent to your room for the first eighteen years of life. Most entering college students have led very narrow, protected, and sheltered social lives.

Most college students come from neighborhoods and schools that are highly segregated by race, religion, and class. While this is true for all groups of students, research shows it is particularly true of white students. If you retreat to the comfort zone of your high school days, it's as if you are locking yourself in your room and imposing a strict curfew on yourself.

In college you have the opportunity to meet a whole range of new people with different backgrounds and different ideas from yours. They may see the world through very different lenses. Get to know how to wear their lenses in addition to your own. It will sharpen your vision.

Look around your classroom. There are twenty-five very interesting and smart people there. Look at the faces in your cafeteria. There are two hundred fifty interesting and smart people there. Get to know these people. Each one has an interesting and inspiring life story that you should hear. And you should hear their stories not because your life story is not exemplary or because you should model any one of them, but rather because all these people should be an important part of your college education. Talk to your college peers. Learn about their experiences and ideas. Check out your own ideas with them. See what they think.

If you come from a big city, you will have the opportunity to meet people from small rural towns. In what ways do they view politics and interpret books differently or the same as you do? If you come from a liberal background, talk to a student whose parents are conservative and find out what that person's perspective is. If you are a student who has to work twenty hours a week just to make tuition payments, get to know someone whose family can afford to fly that student home on weekends. What things do you have in common, and in what ways are your worlds so different that it takes a special effort to speak a common language? Consider taking a friend to attend a cultural event from your background and then go to a cultural event from your friend's background.

Research tells us that students in diverse classrooms learn more deeply and understand issues in a more complex fashion. Students who have embraced the diversity of their colleges are better prepared for participating in a diverse workforce, negotiating contracts with people from different backgrounds, and supervising or being supervised by a wide range of people. Experiencing diversity provides needed expertise for future doctors treating their patients, government leaders discussing global treaties, lawyers working with a variety of clients, and teachers providing quality education to every child in their classrooms. It provides the opportunity for America to realize its highest democratic ideals.

Perhaps most importantly for you as an individual, if you choose to take advantage of the diverse student body of your campus, you are likely to have a much richer and expansive life. Your opportunity for friendship and broad thinking will have no artificial restrictions or boundaries.

6   Develop Good Study Habits

It may come as a surprise that for many students, college success is as much a result of good study skills as it is of intellectual ability or "smarts." That's right. One of the most important keys to academic success in college is having good study skills. Your college already has made the determination that you are intellectually qualified to do good academic work at your school. But translating your intellectual abilities into passing grades requires a fair amount of expertise in the how-to of studying.

Developing good study skills has much to do with knowing yourself and being honest with yourself. There's no single best answer for everyone regarding study skills, but there certainly is a best approach for you as an individual.

Where and under what conditions do you study best? Some students can concentrate quite well in their residence hall rooms with music playing, interruptions and shouts from neighbors, and a generally chaotic setting. Other students need to leave their living space and head to a library or an empty classroom to find the quiet and solitude necessary to concentrate, study, and write.

When you sit down to study, the first thing to do is get yourself organized. Review your assignments. What is due the next day, the next week, the next month? How long is each assignment likely to take? Which assignment are you mentally and physically prepared to focus on first, so that the most difficult assignment will have your deepest concentration. Know whether your study style is to immerse yourself in a single project for hours at a time or to work in twenty- or thirty-minute chunks. Pace yourself. Plan breaks.

Don't allow yourself to get discouraged. It takes time to get acclimated to the pace of work and higher expectations in college. It might take a few assignments to get the hang of it, and you might even get a low grade on a first test or paper that you never even saw in high school. Remember, there's always room to learn from these experiences and to adjust your study schedule and approach as the semester goes along. Don't lose hope over one bad grade or one late night of studying.

In math and science, students often have problem sets to complete daily and weekly and they jump head first into that work. It's certainly essential to keep up with these daily assignments. You definitely want to avoid falling behind and having to race to catch up in those subjects.

There are always some students who believe that while they must keep up with their daily assignments, they can easily put off essays and research papers until a few days or even the night before the due date. Putting off the work of some classes is a certain path to eventual trouble. Writing papers requires a process of thinking, rethinking, drafting, revising, rethinking again, redrafting again, and so on. Every paper you turn in should represent, at the very least, your third draft. And reaching the third draft should represent a process of thinking, composing, and rethinking the content, language, style, and of course technical aspects of the paper.

As you are about to begin on a specific assignment, go back and carefully reread the assignment. It is absolutely frustrating to work for hours on something only to realize that you didn't fully and precisely address the written assignment. Be certain you understand what is expected, and don't hesitate to contact the professor for clarification if you have any questions.

Some students aren't prepared for all the reading required in college courses. It is essential that you learn to read the wide range of text assignments in different ways. Reading history or chemistry textbooks requires a different approach than reading nonfiction or fiction books. Scholarly journal articles and academic monographs require yet another level of focus and concentration to fully comprehend the research findings, empirical analysis, and theoretical discussion they reflect.

Don't sell yourself short in the area of study habits. Do a good, honest assessment of your study habits, and make adjustments and improvements as needed. If you find yourself in need of help in this area, don't hesitate to ask for advice and suggestions very early in your college career.

7 Ask for Help

In high school, asking for academic help is often what distinguishes the kids who are in academic difficulty or considered "at risk" from the "smart" kids. Fortunately, with so many students now taking college preparation courses for SAT, AP, ACT, and other standardized tests, some of the stigma attached to tutoring and asking for assistance has diminished among college-bound students.

In college, the whole notion of asking for academic help is entirely different from high school. Being able to ask for help is crucial, and the first step is admitting to yourself that you should want and need help. Higher education is about scholarly inquiry, and universities are comprised of people who are genuinely interested in discovering, studying, learning, analyzing, creating, and sharing new knowledge. It is in that context that everyone in college, faculty and students alike, are in constant search of deeper, clearer understandings and new insights. If you don't understand the complexities of an argument, you are expected to ask. If you miss the meaning of a lecture, then of course you should ask. If the math assignment or readings are not clear, then without question you should ask.

Your first stop for academic assistance, and it should be a frequent stop, should be with an academic advisor. Advisors know the academic rules for course and graduation requirements. But they also have extensive experience talking and guiding students through their college careers. They will try to help you make decisions about your college plans rather than outline plans for you. After all, this is your college education, not theirs, not your parents', not your teachers', and not your friends'. It is crucial that you figure out what holds most meaning for your studies, your career, and your life. If, for any reason, your advisor is not a good fit for you, then you should have no problem finding a different one.

Many colleges today have different learning labs in which students can just drop in at most hours of the day or night or schedule appointments with specialists. In traditional language labs, there may be a variety of computer programs, software, videos, tutors, and so on. In math labs, students can do their math homework online, using computer programs, working in study groups, or utilizing one-to-one tutorial help. Writing centers have been in place for a long time, helping students conceptualize and organize papers, giving feedback to students on drafts of paper assignments, and assisting students on technical skills such as grammar and composition. More recently, science resource centers have been established to help students in all the science disciplines. Students use computer software designed for specific classes to solve problems, complete homework, and study for exams. Science texts are available for student use, study groups meet at the center, and tutors are on hand for personal assistance.

College libraries are much more comprehensive, sophisticated, and technologically advanced than most neighborhood libraries. College librarians see themselves as teachers and educators and are eager to offer personal assistance to students. Librarians help students learn to access computer databases and find sources in print and online for research papers. They also offer more basic assistance, such as giving tours of the library and helping find books. Most college librarians are on the cutting edge of technological advances and can be of great assistance in helping you get your hands and eyes on the astounding resources available to students and scholars today.

Remember, if you're not asking for help and taking advantage of academic support services, advising, study groups, and tutors, you're not being a smart student. Most of your learning will take place outside of the classroom, and you must be skilled and assertive to be sure your academic learning outside of class is as high quality and intensive as it is inside the classroom.

———

KATIE TOWNSEND — *"Help! I Can't Take Another Four Years of High School!"*

Katie Townsend so looked forward to meeting new friends at college. Like most of the students at her new college, she came from a racially and economically ho-

mogeneous neighborhood and high school, one that was 95% white and upper middle class. She recognized the benefits of meeting people from different backgrounds, and she also was ready to break out of the high school cliques that she had both thrived on and grown very tired of in her senior year.

When Katie arrived for summer orientation, she was excited to meet students from different states and different races. She was placed in a room with, Wendy, a Chinese American student from Washington, D.C., who was very sophisticated, friendly, and bright. Katie and her roommate got along just fine, and even though it wasn't clear they would become best friends, both girls looked forward to building on this new friendship in the fall. Still, Katie felt that she had taken a big first step toward breaking out of her high school mold.

When Katie arrived at college in the fall, she continued to have high expectations. During her school's "welcome days," she met many new students in her residence hall and tried to go to a variety of social activities that were new to her. She went to a lot of fraternity and sorority parties, but she also went to a dance sponsored by the Indian American students that drew hundreds of students and opened her eyes and was lots and lots of fun. Pretty soon, however, Katie's friends from high school who were attending the same college began e-mailing and calling for the old group to get together. Katie missed her friends and was happy to hear from them. Before she knew it, she found herself spending more and more time with her high school friends and was less available to spend time with new people she had met on her floor.

By the second week of classes, Katie was besieged by calls and flyers urging her to participate in sorority rush. Katie's mom and sister had rushed sororities, and she and they had always expected that Katie would rush, too.

At this point Katie was feeling somewhat overwhelmed by all the new things she was encountering at college, and she was feeling a little homesick. Katie found it comforting to hang out with friends from high school amid the familiar talk and social scene that she had always been so good at. She got caught up in the excitement of rush and the comfort of her old friends and decided to join the sorority with her white, relatively wealthy high school crowd. She felt great. Everyone was super nice to Katie, and she spent a lot of time at her sorority for parties and other social functions.

Midway through the first semester, Katie ran into Wendy, her roommate from orientation. They hugged and asked how each was doing. They exchanged e-mail addresses, but Katie knew they would not get in touch. Katie walked away, wondering what had happened to all her plans to break out of her high school mold. She was feeling more settled in college and was getting adjusted to classes and the pressure of homework and tests. She knew her way around the residence hall and campus and was no longer homesick.

On the one hand, everything seemed to be going great; on the other hand, Katie realized she had not grown much. Already, she was tiring of her high school friends and all the parties. Hadn't she done all that for four years in high school? She knew all their stories, jokes, cliques, and gossip. They even all seemed to think alike. She thought about Wendy, about the Indian dance she had attended, and about all the other friendly students in her residence hall who came from all over the country and who had had so many different experiences growing up.

Katie plopped down on her bed and let out a big sigh. Sure, she loved her old friends, but she wanted more from college and from life. It had been all too easy to stay trapped in the same mold and never grow in college. She knew this was not what she wanted. Katie made a commitment to herself that she would not let this happen. Could she have it both ways? She decided to stay with the sorority but to cut back on spending so much of her time there. She decided to join other student organizations. She hung out at night with the kids from her residence hall floor. And she frantically searched for Wendy's e-mail address, sent her a note, and made a date to get together.

8 Discover the Value of Challenging Ideas (Including Your Own)

On the first day of college classes, you are only three months out of high school. Over the course of a single summer, your teachers will stop looking at you as a school child and start seeing you as an adult. This is the time to begin taking responsibility to think and express your own ideas, your own thoughts, and your own opinions.

For years your parents, teachers, and peers have taught you and persuaded you to think and act in particular ways. You've been taught how to interpret history, what books to read, even whom your friends should be. But now it's your turn to be an independent adult thinker. You can assert your own ideas, interpretations, and analyses; read whatever books and authors you like; and make friends and acquaintances with whomever you choose. You also can and should get involved in the issues of the world.

This new stage in your life provides you with tremendous freedom but also bestows significant responsibility on you. Just as you can begin to assert your independence of mind and spirit, you also must be prepared to defend your ideas, opinions, values, decisions, and actions. That can be quite difficult, but you should embrace this opportunity. Don't shy away from it.

During this process of independence taking, try out some new ideas. Think hard. Challenge yourself. Don't let yourself off the hook easily. Be your harshest critic. You'll find that college faculty are expert at critiquing others' points of view. They can pick apart the most complicated argument, analyze and debate theoretical abstractions, and see right through baseless verbiage and undefended ideas. Don't find yourself on the weak side of a critique without having tested out an idea in your mind first. At the same time, don't back off from your own ideas just because someone raises questions for you.

What is so exciting about this process is that you get to explore your own identity and discover the person you really are and will be in your adult life. Why do others think the way they do? Why do some people have such very different political views, social relationships, religious practices, cultural traditions, musical and culinary tastes? Take these years to find the beauty in the way all people see the world. Put yourself in their shoes. Try to understand, as they do, how to make sense of the world—theirs and yours. Learn why they celebrate certain events and policies and challenge, sometimes fiercely, other events and policies.

Then go back into your own shoes and start asking questions. Push others to defend their positions. Push yourself to defend your position. Why do you believe and behave as you do? Is it because others—often people who care deeply for you—have guided you along a certain path? You may be ready now to accept their guidance as your own and continue along that path as a result of your own searching. But you may also decide that you want to set out on a different path or take a different path to what is ultimately the same goal. What's important is that you take responsibility and ownership of your life and your society and begin to set forth on a journey that is distinctly yours.

In the classroom as in your life journey, it is also time to ask hard questions. Challenge your professors about what they tell you as fact or what they offer as interpretation. How did they come to that opinion? Look for the evidence and the research behind their analysis. Do the careful reading that is essential to asking good questions. Challenge the authors that you read. Become a critical and serious thinker. Be thoughtful in your self-reflection, and be critical in your questioning the ideas, assertions, and analyses that others thrust upon you.

9   Live a Balanced Life

Balance is a core principle for having a successful college experience.

It is crucial to take care of your mind AND body while you're in college. The stress and intensity are very real, and it's important to remember to eat and to eat well, to find time for sleeping, working out, laughing, smiling, and so on. It's good to "get away" from the college environment at least twice a month, even if it's just for an hour or two. Go to the nearest downtown, watch a movie off campus, work on a community service project that takes you off campus, take a long walk, go home.

Treat yourself with respect. You deserve it. (And, by the way, treat your peers with the very same level of respect.) Don't abuse your body by not eating or sleeping. Be careful about substance abuse. Don't entrust your body to alcohol. Be as smart about your life style as you are about classes if you want to remain competitive in college and in your profession. Avoid drugs. Why do you need any of this? You're a bright, high-achieving person with your whole adult life ahead of you. Don't blow it. Don't allow someone to do violence to you, verbally or physically, and don't allow violence to enter your environment.

Work out. Take walks. Go to the gym to lift weights, shoot hoops, or join an intramural team. Dress appropriately. If it's raining or snowing outside, carry an umbrella and wear a hat and gloves. Eat three meals a day. Complain about dorm food if you must, but there's always plenty to eat and enough variety to find something you like.

If you're feeling sick, go to the college's health service. Really, don't mess around with your health. Rest a lot. Eat chicken or miso soup and other foods that will help heal you. Drink fluids. Smile and laugh a bit. Your body is telling you to slow down and take care of yourself. Listen carefully, because sometimes your body is smarter than your brain.

10 Remember That Tomorrow Will Be Even Better than Today

The adrenaline rush in the first year of college is perhaps unequaled at any other point in one's life. The highs and lows of classes and the ups and downs of social relationships are as exulting as they can seem devastating. It's about growing up, intense learning and study, independence, and the onset of adulthood. It's about all the new people you are meeting and all the new ideas you are confronting. Some are glorious and provoke highs you haven't ever felt before. And, at the same time, other moments are sad, depressing, and painful. Know that you'll always get past the tough moments.

There is the move up to campus, meeting the new roommate, taking the first exam, writing the first paper, going to the first football game in the fall. Some days will be never-ending, seeming to go on forever and ever. And then there will be a broken relationship, a critical comment from a professor, a bad phone call from home, a rejection, a conflict with the college bureaucracy. How could it get so bad, you will wonder in your tears? And, then, before your tears have dried, there is an invitation in the mail, an A on a quiz, a quiet walk across campus, admission into a summer internship. All of this and it's only the second week of college! How could this be?

Take it one day at a time and cherish each moment (except the forgettable ones—learn from those moments and then forget them forever). Keep a diary, take pictures, store the best experiences in your permanent memory bank. Write down your best ideas for tomorrow and for the long term. Tomorrow will be here before you know it. Trust that you'll quickly get past the trying moments. Make the good days last a lifetime, as your smile, laughter, and good ideas make the world a better place for all of us.

Who Am I? Discovering Yourself and Your Identity

11   Decide Who You Are—It's *Your* Life Now

Now it's your turn. For better or worse—actually, it's all for the better—college is a time when you make the transition from teenager to adult, from boy to man, from girl to woman. You begin to make your own rules. You get to decide your own values. Most importantly, you get to create your own opportunities and take responsibility for your own mistakes.

The knowledge that you are in charge of your life can be both thrilling and frightening. That's how freedom is. That's what the journey of life is about. You can stay up all night, live on a diet that consists of ice cream only, skip all your classes. But is that the life you want? Well, it's your choice, for good or for bad. Now, when you break the rules, they are your rules. And when you set forth on your own path, it's your path and choices, your accomplishments and failures, and the meaning and fulfillment are your own.

One interesting manifestation of this change takes place in the clothing choices of college students. When high school students come to campus for their college tours and interviews, they often take on the "look" of what they believe to represent adulthood. Students are smartly dressed, and all wear up-to-date fashions. These seventeen-year-old high school students look like they are the graduating college seniors or older.

Fast forward one year to the first-year college students. Both men and women are less aware of their appearance and of the latest styles. What's going on? In high school, students are trying to act like they are adults because they know they aren't yet, so they need to make more effort to dress the part. In college, however, students truly are beginning to be adults in thought and action, and thus they needn't dress up to fill the part because they are playing the adult role legitimately. As adults, they have the freedom to dress up or down as the situation dictates without worrying quite so much about putting on pretenses.

Without a doubt, parents and teachers and clergy and friends will still all be trying to advise you and influence your decisions and your life's journey. Listen carefully to what they say, because they mean well, have a lifetime of experience to share with you, and can serve as important resources and support for you. But, ultimately, this is your time now. Enjoy the experience of growing up, becoming an adult, and being grown up. Every year will be different and exciting. Enjoy and cherish every moment!

12   Discover Your Values

Who am I? What is the meaning of life? What am I doing here at this college?

The weight of important existential questions of life can feel like a heavy burden in the first year of college, but they are essential for moving forward in life. Indeed, it is critical that you start the process of questioning during college.

I often ask my first-year students to write essays about their individual and group identities. My students embrace this assignment because it allows them to look back on their experiences and reflect on their values, their ideals, and their identities. They write outstanding papers for this assignment, and I advise you to do the same. But, invariably, they will ask me how I can possibly grade them on their identity. I tell them that I value each one of my students as an A+ person, an extraordinary individual, with a unique and exceptional life story. But I grade the essay, not the person. It is the ability of each student to tell their story in the most thoughtful and reflective manner that will determine their grade.

That's what I would say to you, too. During the first year of college, you should begin in earnest to shape and tell the story of what you find when you look deeply inside to discover who you are now and who you want to be in your lifetime. The deeper you allow yourself to probe and explore, the better able you will be to move with a strong foundation into adulthood. Don't be concerned if the answers aren't easily or immediately found. This is a process that should and does take time.

This process of introspection almost without exception does begin to take place in earnest during the college years, so it's best for you to take control of it. You will find yourself with a whole new set of people surrounding you, new friends, new classmates, new teachers, new adults. With these new people and surroundings, you have a unique opportunity to explore, experiment, establish, and assert who you are, what your identity is, and who you want to be in life.

In college you will find that you have much, much more unstructured free time on your hands than you have ever experienced before. While for some people the opportunity to constantly be busy is very worthwhile, having at least some time on your hands can be very useful in giving you a chance to think about your purpose in life, your values, and your identity.

13 Determine What You Like (and Dislike) in Life

One of the most exciting opportunities of adulthood is identifying those things that you like and don't like. This has been an ongoing process since you were very young, but you were always making choices in the context of your parents and other adults setting the parameters of your choices and influencing your decisions.

To make choices of your own requires being open to trying "new" things so you have a broad enough experience to make good choices for yourself. It also means stepping back and seeing all the "old" things you've been doing in your life with new eyes and perspectives.

Your likes and dislikes come in many shapes and forms, big and small, significant and less significant. For instance, at college you get to decide what toothpaste to use at the sink and what soap and shampoo to use in the shower. You get to decide what food you want to eat at every meal—all sugar all the time, fried or baked, milk or coffee, tofu or steak, green beans or green Jell-O.

You get to choose how to groom yourself and what clothes to wear each day. Do you want a crew cut, Afro, shaved head, or full, flowing tresses? Do you want to grow a beard or be clean shaven? Will you wear jeans or skirts to class? Will you choose ripped pants or ironed shirts? Will you try wild patterns that call attention or bland colors that don't? Your parents may have strong views about all of these choices, but now you are on your own and they are your decisions.

You get to choose classes you want each semester and then decide on your major. Many people will tell you what you should study, and most colleges will impose requirements that limit your choices. Still, despite what your parents, academic advisors, and friends suggest, it's up to you to make the selections that make most sense to you.

The same holds true for almost every aspect of your life. You decide how hard you want to study for your exams, whether to read the assigned and/or recommended readings, and how much effort you want to put into class papers. You choose whether to play sports and whether to attend intercollegiate football or field hockey games on campus. Will you go to Cancun for spring break or do community service through Alternative Spring Break? You get to choose your friends. You get to decide whether or not to drink alcohol and/or get drunk. You get to decide if you want to use drugs. You choose where and with whom you want to live. Will you raise money for the homeless shelter or spend money for new clothes? Will you choose to run for student government office or decide you never want to read a newspaper? Will you decide to rush a fraternity or choose to stay far away from the Greek houses? Will you stay up all night or go to bed at eleven o'clock?

Ultimately, these questions are about the kind of person you want to be. College offers you a chance to reaffirm the choices you've been making in the first part of your life or to put those aside and try out some new choices. If you do this right, it will be a continual process that lasts throughout your lifetime. Give yourself time and space to do this. Most of all, give yourself the power to shape your own life.

BOBBY JACKSON—*"I've Got an Opinion about That!"*

In Bobby Jackson's home, his father set the rules. He was a man of strong values and a strong will, and no one was about to challenge him. And, with such a strong adult in the house, no one ever thought about asking Bobby for his opinion.

Sometimes, however, Bobby rebelled against his father because he got tired of his father always thinking he was right, and the two of them had at times exchanged some strong words. For Bobby, it hardly mattered to him what his father said or what they were fighting about; he just got into the habit of being contrary, especially with his father. So Bobby came to college with a penchant for rebelling and arguing when the mood hit him.

Bobby was amazed the first day he passed through the campus commons. Students were passing out flyers and speaking through megaphones about all kinds of issues. They seemed just like his dad—strident, self-assured, strong willed, and completely certain they were 100% right. Bobby hated their cockiness but kept his mouth shut—after all, he was just a first-year student.

But Bobby kept meeting students who felt so strongly about all kinds of issues. There was something stimulating about the debates and the issues. Although Bobby didn't really know too many of the issues, he knew from his fights with his father that he could be a pretty strident critic of others' viewpoints.

Bobby decided to enter the fray one day while he was passing through the commons. As one student was loudly exhorting the students going by on their way to class, Bobby paused and let the student know how stupid he thought his views were. Rather than act defensively, which was what Bobby clearly expected based on his experience with his father, this student invited Bobby to offer an alternative explanation and answer to the problem they were debating.

Bobby was stunned. No one had ever asked him for his opinion. Bobby's father had opinions and his father had taught him what he should believe. But

Bobby had never really thought through any issues for himself. Bobby staggered off to class, for once his mouth shut.

For Bobby, this was one of those existential, life-altering experiences one reads about in books or sees in the movies. But this was no movie. Bobby didn't know what he believed in. He had always done just what his father had told him—or the exact opposite just to spite him. What were his views about politics and world events? Why did he follow a certain religion and not another? What did he want to do with his life? What did he really care about? Why was he even in college—how did he get there without even knowing what he wanted to study or do professionally?

Bobby was both forlorn and exhilarated at the same time—forlorn because he had never before thought for himself about his life and values, exhilarated because here was his opportunity to do so. Bobby didn't know what to do with himself.

For starters, Bobby decided not to be so critical and outspoken, and he began to listen to others' views more closely. He also dug out a high school graduation gift he thought he'd never use—a journal. Each day he began to write down what he believed in. He was amazed at all of the contradictions and inconsistencies in his views and arguments, but after a while, he began to find himself.

Bobby was no longer merely a critic, a responder, with no views of his own. He found he was beginning to carve out his own meaning in life, his own set of values, his own direction, his own worldview. Sometimes his values overlapped with his dad's, and sometimes his views were quite different—but whatever the case, these were his own views. Bobby was taking control of his life, and was he ever excited about his future! He started to get involved in campus organizations and politics, and by sophomore year, there he was, handing out flyers and exhorting the new college students to join his political group.

14 Find Your Voice and Take a Stand

Kids have opinions from a very young age, and they know how to express themselves. Though it's usually about very personal issues—needing a nap, wanting a diaper changed, being hungry—they're quick to let you know what they're thinking.

Over the next eighteen years, however, through parenting, schooling, and other socializing institutions, children and especially teenagers are taught not to have their own opinions. They're told it's rude to disagree with an adult. Their teachers tell them over and over again not to invoke a personal view into papers or to use the first person *I*. The first person is essentially prohibited in most high schools—no *I*, no opinions, no viewpoint, no personal positions—leave that to the adults, the teachers, the experts.

Along comes college, and suddenly professors are asking you for your opinion and expecting you to have one! "How does your personal experience inform the theory of this author?" your professor will ask. You will be asked to write in the first person. You will be challenged to rediscover the *I* in your vocabulary and thought processes.

As you walk across the college campus, students will confront you about your views on the upcoming election—who are you voting for, and why? They will want to know your opinion about foreign affairs. They will ask you to join a demonstration for or against a civil rights issue. You will be invited to a talk by a conservative or liberal speaker and will be expected to know who the speaker is and whether you support his or her view or not.

You will be asked about religion—about organized religious institutions and more generally about faith and spirituality. You will be questioned about the ethnic joke or gender joke you make at someone's expense. It may have sounded funny and harmless at the high school lunch table, but now, in college, you may be challenged to consider and defend the sensibility of that humor.

There will be campus issues you'll be expected to think about, too. Is tuition too high? Should there be a student-run bookstore? Do you support a "safe walk" program on campus? Should professors give final exams before the last day of class? What hours should be set for quiet time on your residence hall floor? Should the cafeteria offer whole wheat bread or white?

These questions may seem overwhelming and yet very exciting at the same time. What if you don't know enough to have an informed opinion? How do you learn about these things? What if you don't care or never cared before? What if you care really deeply and want to become a leader of one of these groups?

Everyone in society is trying to tell us what we should believe. There are loads of sound-bite answers to complex questions in society that truly require clear, critical, and complex answers. As a college-educated person, you will want to understand the complexities of issues and to arrive at answers that go beyond traditional, simplistic solutions. The starting point is to realize that your opinion matters and that society needs you to have that opinion. Don't let others form your views for you. Your view and your voice matter.

15 Learn to Enjoy Yourself, Learning, and the College Experience

Your life will be much more fulfilling and satisfying if you learn to enjoy who you are and what you do.

You have four or more years of college ahead of you, an intensive learning focus throughout college, and, in the years beyond, a lifetime of being with yourself. All of that will be a lot more pleasant if you can find the secret of happiness at college, in your learning, and with yourself.

You need to be clear that happiness is not always a ball of laughter. Happiness is not the same as partying. It is important that you be clear about what is meaningful and fulfilling in your life. Money alone or A grades by themselves will not necessarily bring you happiness or enjoyment.

In college, you should focus on both the outcome and the process. One outcome is that you will obtain a degree at the end. A second outcome is that you will be a well-educated person. A third outcome is that you will be prepared to be an active and engaged participant in your community in a diverse democracy. A fourth outcome is that you have become an independent adult. You should feel good if you're making progress toward those goals.

It's equally important, however, that you learn to enjoy the process of getting to those outcomes. Much of the college experience centers on learning. If you focus only on your grades and not on what you are learning, you may achieve your ultimate goal but be a very unhappy person along the way. If you find classes boring and studying drudgery, you're in trouble. You want to develop a love of learning. You want to look forward to the intellectual energy of a class discussion with faculty and peers; the exposure to new ideas, perspectives, and discoveries in course readings and assignments; and the intrinsic intellectual thrill every time you gain a new insight.

You can worry too much about tests so that you are miserable even when you do well. You can stress constantly about your grade point average so that you are never satisfied or fulfilled, even with perfection. You can be so obsessed with the outcome of graduating from college that you never enjoy the beauty of attending college.

The same holds true for enjoying yourself. You need to learn to live comfortably and amicably with yourself. You need to find pleasure and satisfaction in your thoughts, values, actions, and outlook. You need to feel good about yourself, about how you are continuing to develop and grow, and about your abilities to change those areas you want to improve.

You may set goals for yourself, but if you don't enjoy the path to achieving the goals, the successful outcome may not bring you the satisfaction you desire. In college, you want to learn about yourself so you can be a person you like and admire. You want to learn how to enjoy the process of learning because so much of your time and energy will be spent learning. You want to be happy about earning your college degree, but you also want to enjoy the experience of getting your college education.

16 Take (Safe) Risks

College is a time to step out, take chances, and find your true personal, academic, and professional interests. It's a time of experimentation, reflection, and affirmation.

When we hear about risk taking, it is usually associated with what are clearly negative actions. Risky behavior is often translated as experimenting with illicit drugs, driving under the influence, or having unprotected sexual relations. Those behaviors are not risky—they are downright stupid and dangerous.

Taking risks means moving out of your comfort zone. It means stretching your range of friendships, expanding your intellectual horizons, and exploring the world of opportunities that lie before you.

If you've felt terribly constrained at home and in high school, don't go to college and break out of your shell by going crazy the first week or semester. Be smart, and take your time and err on the safe side of risk taking. And if you feel the need to rebel against your parents or other authorities in your life, don't harm yourself in the process. Be smart and do better than them. Set an example by how you choose to live your life as an adult.

Did you grow up listening to a particular type of music? Rock? Rap? Country? Classical? College is a time to borrow a friend's CD, go to the opera, or go to a club that plays music you've never really allowed yourself to be open to.

Do you like Italian or Mexican food? In college, try some salmon, tofu, hummus, or tea. Taste some new varieties of ice cream. Go to an Indian restaurant. Try a new salad dressing or a different kind of mustard on your hot dog.

You've spent the last four years managing the complex cliques and social arrangements of high school in order to fit in. Now relax, forget all that stuff, and be yourself. Make some new friends. Hang out with people whom it wasn't cool to be friends with in high school but who could very likely turn out to be your best friends.

Wear clothes that you like, not that your friends all wear or your parents liked. Try something bright, or a different color, or a new style. Buy a new hat or scarf.

The same is true about your academic interests. Don't just get busy filling requirements—take some courses you like. Did you always want to know more about paintings in the art museum? Study art history. Have you wanted to feel like you can understand the business section of the newspaper? Take an economics course. Was your favorite school assignment that of collecting different kinds of leaves in second grade? Then take a biology class or environmental studies or geology—all of those fields might bring you back to an original intellectual passion.

Every day on television we are faced with innumerable choices about which toothpaste or laundry detergent to use, yet when it comes to professional careers, most college students think their options are limited to business, law, engineering, and medicine. What a shame!

This is your life and your profession! You get to decide what makes you happy, what gives you meaning in life, what you want to spend forty and usually many more hours of every week of the next fifty years doing. Don't let other people—be it well-meaning parents, teachers, friends, or some imaginary voices in your consciousness—tell you what to do with your life and your time. By all means, listen to these people, because they do mean well and do have your best interests at heart. But college is the time to explore a life of opportunities in any number of professions that are open to someone as bright and as interesting as you!

17 Make Quality Friendships

Surround yourself with good people. Choose to be close friends with people you can trust and who will care about your well-being. Look at their values and judgments. Be sure you respect them.

Good friends make all the difference in the world. Of course, you can and will have a great many acquaintances, and it's best not to have just an inner circle of friends. Be open to interacting with and learning from all different kinds of people. And when you choose your close friends, pick good people. It will hold you in good stead throughout your life.

At the same time, don't be overly picky. In college you will meet hundreds or even thousands of other students. You might find that you don't particularly like many of them. That's okay. If your school had two thousand students and you don't like, say, fifteen hundred of them (though that's pretty hard to imagine), don't go around thinking you can't find anyone you like. You've just identified five hundred students that you could very well like very much. Multiply that by ten times or more if you go to a very large university, and you might be complaining that you don't like as many as fifteen thousand students on campus. Guess what? That still leaves you with five thousand great people out of which to find a few friends.

Part of the trick of finding friends is by being a "friend-ly" person yourself. All that means is that you need to allow yourself to be liked by others. That doesn't mean you have to be Ms. Popularity or Mr. Smiley Face all the time. But it does mean that you should say hello back to people who smile at you, that you should go out with people who invite you to go out with them (at least some of the time), that you should share a little about yourself and open yourself to the possibility of liking others and having others like you.

The other thing about friends is to remember that relationships take work and time. You probably have a pretty good idea of how much time it takes to do well in a class you're taking. Good friendships demand the same—effort and time. Friends should be there for you when you need them, but you need to be there for them, too, even at inconvenient times. Relationships take time to grow; they require hanging out and doing things together and building a wealth of experiences together.

If you surround yourself with good people, they will give you good advice. They will steer you in good directions. They will set high expectations for your behavior and values. They will not get you into dangerous situations or ask you to do things you know to be wrong. You will become a better person for those friendships, as will your friends.

JENNIFER LANDERS—*"Taming the Party Animal."*

Jennifer Landers comes from a wealthy, sophisticated family. She is popular, pretty, and social. She's known to her friends from home as a silly, fun girl with one mystery—she also gets good grades. When she was admitted to an elite university, her "stretch" school, her friends, counselors, and even her parents were very surprised, to put it mildly. Jennifer just laughed off all the jokes but followed along in their social expectations. She spent a lot of time and money on new clothes for college and talked with her friends incessantly about what sorority she would pledge and how much she looked forward to college partying.

After a long summer of waiting for the start of college, the first day of classes arrived, and Jennifer was terrified. Faculty handed out syllabi with difficult readings and long papers due almost immediately. Although Jennifer publicly

kept up her pretense of the silly, social girl at first, she also knew she had to con-
front her doubts. She knew there was no way that a party girl could succeed at
this school. And she had already met so many smart, serious students at orien-
tation that she questioned whether she should just give up—leave college and fly
home. But Jennifer also knew that she was smart. Her teachers had told her that
she was an excellent writer. She knew how to study for exams. She had strong de-
termination to be a successful, professional woman and understood the necessity
of doing well in college.

Jennifer tried to play it both ways during her first semester. She did act like the
silly, party girl on weekends but tried her hardest when she went back to her room
to study and be prepared for class. One of her professors noted on a paper,
"Jennifer, this is an outstanding, analytic paper. I wish you would share more
of your good insights in class instead of talking and giggling so much. You have
so much to contribute." When the semester came to a close, Jennifer decided that
it was time for her to find a better balance in her life, to shake the "silly" facade
(yet still find time to have fun), and to start living her life, both inwardly and
outwardly, as the more confident, serious person she knew she was.

Jennifer saw that she could fairly easily pass her courses with Bs and Cs, but
she knew she was much better than that. The next semester she enrolled in more
difficult courses and spent more time on her studies and less on parties, though
she still had an active social life on weekends. She appreciated that her profes-
sors noticed, her parents praised her, and her friends still liked her. Jennifer felt
good about herself, her future, and how well she was managing the different as-
pects of her life as an intelligent woman and young adult.

18   Rediscover Your Place in Your Family

Can you imagine what it would be like to have an adult relationship with your parent(s)?

Life at home had its rules and routines. You knew where you stood in family matters. You were the child to your mother and/or father, growing up and experiencing life through the developmental stages of childhood and adolescence, but they were still always the adult(s) and you were not.

Now, in college, you are fast becoming an adult, just like your mother and/or father. It is a time when you can and should refashion your relationship with your parents from that of child to adult to that of adult to adult.

Certainly you will always be the child of your parent(s), but now it is time to start making the transition from being just the child to being the adult child, the adult friend, the independent adult in relationship with your parent(s).

This is not to say that you shouldn't still look to your parents for comfort if you're having a bad day or call excitedly to tell them that your professor praised you for completing a great lab experiment or to report that you have a new boyfriend.

This good transition is not likely to happen overnight, but you should want your relationship to take some big steps forward over the course of your college education. It will happen when you shift from having your parents make decisions for you to asking them for advice so that you can make your own decisions. It will happen when you make your own decision about your major, course choices, how to study for tests, whom to date, setting a curfew, balancing your bank account, paying your taxes, cooking your own meals, and so on.

You will see the change when you come home for vacations or when you decide to spend your vacations with your friends and not your family. It will happen when you make an important and difficult decision even though it is one that your parents would not agree with.

Not only are you growing and changing in this relationship, but so, too, are your parent(s). They may have even more difficulty with this than you do. They're not used to your not living at home or to not being able to tell you what to do, or they may think of you as a child only, not as an adult child or an adult friend.

If both of you work hard at this, as you must do with all your important relationships, you and your parent(s) will realize the beauty of your new relationship, which is more mature, equal, and meaningful. Both you and your parent(s) may have to leave some familiar history and ways of relating behind you, and you may find the path to change filled with some conflicts, disagreements, and trying to hold onto the past. In the long run, though, you will happily look forward to an ever deeper and more loving relationship in the many decades that lie before you.

19 Get Comfortable Being Alone

The high school routine is all about being busy—superbusy. Take difficult classes. Join extracurricular activities. Get a job. Do volunteer work. Help around the house. Spend time with friends—when you have a free minute. Everyone is rewarded for being an active, busy person. It helps on your college applications, it brings praise from teachers and parents, and it makes you feel good because you believe you're doing the "right" thing by being so busy.

But what's missing in that picture? The missing ingredient is *you*, and the time to be alone with the very wonderful person you have become. If you really believe the tips in this book, then you'll believe that you're a pretty extraordinary person! So, if you had the opportunity to be with someone as special as you are, wouldn't you jump at that chance in a second?!

There is great value to being alone with yourself. It gives you a moment to pause and reflect. It gives you time to wind down, to relax, to reevaluate, to think, and to contemplate the world. It allows you to do nothing.

What can you do when you are alone with yourself? You can listen to music or even make music. You can be quiet. You can go for a walk. You can lie in your bed and close your eyes—or lie there and stare up at the ceiling. You can review the past day, your relationships, your classes, your conversations. You can watch TV. You can go to a movie. You can go to an event on campus by yourself. You can eat a meal by yourself. You can do nothing.

Sometimes the act of doing nothing allows you to do the most. It can free the clutter from your mind so that you can think clearly. Sometimes silence is necessary to allow you to hear yourself think. Sometimes closing your eyes allows you to see more clearly than ever before. Sometimes being alone will help you be an even better friend to those you care about and like to be around.

The one requirement to being alone is that you must like yourself. And if you don't like yourself, then the discomfort you feel when you are alone is a wake-up call to get in touch with yourself so you can begin to become a person you can like a whole lot more. No one wants to spend much time with someone they don't like. That holds true even for ourselves. Find that special individual inside you, and you will discover one of your very best lifelong friends.

20 Fall in Love

This isn't Hollywood we're talking about. This is your life. Love is one of life's wonderful blessings, and you may very well experience it during your college years.

One thing Hollywood often neglects to tell us is that love is tied to relationships, and relationships are difficult arrangements that require a great deal of attention. You must be prepared to cherish and nurture your loving relationships.

When your favorite romantic movie ends after two hours, it feels as if the story will go on forever. But after the first two hours of your loving relationship, guess what? You don't get to leave the movie theater and live happily ever after in fantasyland. There you and your partner are in full living color, ready or not, with all the challenges and thrills that loving relationships bring us. That's both the good news and the bad news.

With falling in love in college, the reality is that it oftentimes comes with disappointment. Just as love takes you to the farthest reaches of joy and happiness, breaking up with someone you truly love can be deeply sad and painful. And college love and relationships, because they take place at a relatively young age and in unique settings, are usually not the kind that last forever, even though they may be intensely felt and deeply joyous and fulfilling. The good news is that you will almost certainly find other loving relationships; the bad news is that the time of breaking up can hurt and can be distressing and distracting.

When you fall in love in college, it's important to remember that you're still in college. Oh yeah—college. Did you forget already? Enjoy your love, but still find time to do your homework, study for tests, and write research papers. Your heart may be floating, but keep your mind grounded in the real world. Life goes on, as do your classes and your professors' assignments.

Love and relationships require taking risks. They are most certainly worth the risk that the love won't be requited or that the relationship won't be lasting. You would never want to miss out on the joy of a deeply felt loving relationship. Just keep in mind the opportunity this provides to learn how to incorporate love and relationships into your daily life and other responsibilities, commitments, and cares. Do remember throughout that you're still a college student!

Getting the Most out of College

21 Make Yourself a Part of the Scholarly Community

College connotes different things to different people. I hope you'll be one of those students who thinks of college as a community—or, more specifically, a scholarly community—in which you get to spend four years of your life with a group of people who are deeply engaged with ideas, exploration, questioning, discovery, analysis, and problem solving. To do so will most definitely put you in the right mind-set for a successful college experience.

Consider for a moment some other ideas about college. For some students, college is like an extended summer camp where the primary goal is to make great friends, party, and have as much fun as possible while you pick up a degree along the way. For others, it is a professional training ground where you are preparing for a lucrative career. Still others think of it as a place of competition and endless judgment, with tests and exams and grades.

Why do I encourage you to approach your college experience as a scholarly community? Let's take the community aspect first. It's important to surround yourself with good people. As you grow and develop personally, socially, and intellectually, it's so much healthier to do so in a supportive environment of thinking, caring people. It is in this sense of community that college is far more than a set of requirements or courses or credits to complete. You have the unique opportunity to think, study, and grow surrounded by and engaged with other bright, thinking people.

In terms of the scholarly aspect of college, it's important that you begin to self-identify as a young scholar or a scholar apprentice. This piece of advice is not intended to pigeonhole you or limit you socially—in fact, it will probably do just the opposite. It will prevent you from becoming overly parochial by allowing you to grow and expand exponentially.

Personal and social growth is, of course, essential, but what makes college unique is the attention to analytic thinking, books, lectures, discussions, critical insights, discoveries, and information. You have the opportunity to be a part of and contribute to a collection of people, faculty and students alike, who are focused on learning, exploring, and thinking deeply about all sorts of issues and topics and inquiries.

Once you've received your letter of admission to college, it's actually very easy to become a part of the scholarly community. The hardest part is to make a shift in your mind-set. Instead of thinking of course work as a series of assignments, tests, and homework, you need to think of it as a great opportunity for learning. Instead of thinking of your teachers as people who judge you and have control of grading, imagine them as mentors, fellow thinkers, senior colleagues, and scholarly friends and allies. Look at bulletin boards or the school newspaper and attend the daily guest lectures and talks on campus. Go to theater productions, art exhibits, and classical concerts. Read national and global newspapers. Peruse scientific and popular magazines that address intellectual issues. Visit faculty in their offices. Go to receptions, book signings, and poetry readings. Hang out with your friends in your residence hall late at night and talk about an exciting or controversial idea from your class that day.

22 Think Critically

Okay, so you know what it means to think, and you've been doing a lot of hard work throughout high school that required you to think. So why would this be one of this book's tips, and why would you need to be concerned about critical thinking in college?

Consider what sets apart those who are college educated from those who are not. It is the expectation that a college-educated person will think insightfully and analytically about issues and can get to the root of the complex questions and challenges that face us personally and as a society.

Thinking critically is one of the most essential lessons of college. And, unfortunately, in high school, too few students are asked to think critically—even those who score very well on standardized tests, write well-organized essays on exams, and quickly complete advanced math assignments.

Critical thinking means that you are able to consider and analyze ideas, readings, debates, and discoveries in a comprehensive and thorough manner. It means that you can understand the nuances of an author's ideas and then cogently challenge those ideas. It means that you can understand a point of view and then critique that point of view from multiple perspectives. It means you can hold several compelling but competing ideas and arguments in your mind at the same time and then examine the strengths and weaknesses of each. It means that you're usually impatient with two-sided debates because you realize that most issues have more than two sides and that most issues are far more complex than the discussion that any debate format will elicit. It means that you ask difficult questions of yourselves, others, and the physical world around you and that when you find reasonable answers to your questions, you ask a second and third set of questions that probe more broadly and more deeply.

Some of my supposedly best prepared students, those who come from well-heeled suburban and private high schools, turn in for their first college papers work that is clear and well organized but unfortunately don't have much substance. They just don't say much. In high school they were praised and rewarded for such papers, but in college they will be expected to do much more. These papers have good form but insufficient substance and analysis. These students too often haven't been challenged to think critically. By contrast, I have other students whose rural or urban high schools are not so highly ranked and whose paper writing skills are sometimes lacking, but in their lives they have somehow been forced to ask difficult questions and to analyze and challenge normative assumptions in deeper ways.

Both sets of students (of course, these groupings are overly broad generalizations) will have considerable work to do in college. The good news is that they all have the ability to think critically. The problem is that until college, few have been asked to do so.

The best approach to thinking critically is to ask questions to peel back layers of understandings. You should ask these questions about your own ideas, assumptions, and life, and you should also ask them about the ideas of others you meet through novels, articles, textbooks, and lectures. Go back again and again to probe and analyze. Accept your professors' feedback and perhaps initial lower grades with open arms, because what they are doing is challenging you to raise your self-expectations for your work.

If you had already finished your learning and intellectual development, you wouldn't need to be in college. Learning to think critically will permit you to lead and excel in so many personal, intellectual, civic, and professional fields. It's one of the greatest gifts of a good college education.

23 Ask Questions

Ever since first grade, teachers have been telling you that there is no such thing as a bad question. And yet you know in your heart that they never, ever, meant it. For as soon as those words would come out of your teacher's mouth, some innocent, believing student in class would raise his hand and then get ridiculed for asking just that—a "bad" question.

I can't promise you that you won't be ridiculed by faculty, family, and friends for asking questions, but I can tell you that if you don't ask questions, and lots of them, you might as well not be in college.

Questioning is at the core of intellectual life. It comes from basic human curiosity. Its source is our need to explore what isn't yet understood, discover the unknown, examine the truths behind the truth, and develop the capacity to see from multiple perspectives. Questioning allows our social and scientific worlds to advance from one generation to the next.

Asking questions is also a very practical matter. You need to know where your class is going to be held so you can be there on time on the first day of class. You need to know whether classes start on the hour, on the half hour, or at ten minutes past the hour. You want to know how to address a professor, by their title or by their first name. You need to know when your first exam is due, and what your professor thinks about using Web sites as sources for research papers. You most certainly will need to ask how to access the rich virtual and print resources of your library.

Similarly, in your personal life, some of you will need to learn how to do your laundry. Some students will need to learn about opening a bank account and balancing a checkbook. You will need to learn where the public bathrooms are throughout the campus. You will need to know what to do when you're standing in the hall in your bathrobe after taking a shower and you realize you've locked yourself out of your residence hall room.

Questioning is also political. Asking the question is a statement that you have the right and the responsibility to question authorities and to question authority. You have the right to ask the department chair why your professor does not hold office hours or frequently misses classes. You have the responsibility to ask the president of your college why the faculty does not include more tenured women. You have the right to challenge the news media's depiction of current events. You have the responsibility to ask students at your lunch table in the residence hall cafeteria why they are laughing at racist jokes. You have the responsibility to ask why more students are not voting in campus elections for student leaders or in national presidential and congressional elections.

It's true that some questions will irritate, agitate, and complicate your life and others' lives. But that doesn't mean that the questions are "bad" ones. Just keep asking your questions—that's the role of the scholar.

<hr/>

JOHN WAKEFIELD—*"Is That Really True?"*

John Wakefield came to college in awe of his professors. After all, hadn't all the college admissions literature talked about how smart, articulate, and renowned they were? He had held his high school teachers in high regard, and while some of them were truly excellent, he felt that some just didn't know what they were talking about. His college professors had Ph.D.s and wrote books—that sure seemed credentials enough to John.

John also believed what he read in textbooks. Weren't you supposed to? He couldn't even imagine that textbooks could have a particular perspective or hold a certain point of view—or even be wrong. It all seemed pretty straightforward to John—you go to college to study with brilliant professors and learn all about your major from informative texts.

John's first weeks of college went just as he had expected. The professor handed out a clear and challenging syllabus, readings were assigned, and homework and tests were scheduled throughout the semester. John went to the college bookstore to buy the assigned books for all his classes. Some students complained about the course load and the amount of studying they had to do, but John came to college expecting to do a lot of studying and wasn't worried about it.

In science class one day, the professor had students turn to page 40 of the textbook and asked what they thought of the information and explanation presented. The students were mostly quiet, except for those few who always raised their hands. But the professor wasn't satisfied with their comments—she said that there was an alternative explanation that challenged what the text was presenting as fact. John was surprised that the textbook wouldn't be up to date, but he thought that this just showed how brilliant his professor was. Students discussed the alternative explanation and offered a variety of comments to demonstrate why it now seemed preferable to the textbook information.

Then the professor said that she didn't accept the alternative explanation either. And, she went on, she didn't have a good explanation in place of either of those that had been presented thus far, but stated that this confusion was exactly what made science interesting to her. John and his classmates were confused—of all his classes, science had been the most clear, definitive, and unquestioned.

In sociology, John thought he did perfectly on his first paper. He had carefully read the texts for class and taken copious notes. But the professor in that class wrote all over the paper, asking why John believed what he had written. The professor wanted to know why John just accepted different authors' opinions as fact. Hadn't John heard the professor challenge the authors' theories and perspectives? The professor wanted John's opinion, and he wanted John to make strong arguments to support his point of view.

This was all new to John. He was skilled at taking notes, reading carefully, and writing up in papers and tests what he thought professors wanted to hear. In his high school, which was first rate, John had been rewarded for this skill, and he was a straight-A student. Now he was no longer the straight-A student, and his professors were requiring him to think critically and independently. This was new and difficult for John, but he quickly came to see that this was what his professors loved to do for themselves.

John began to see that to do well in college, he needed to learn to challenge the information and ideas, arguments, and opinions that were all around him, including his own. This was hard, at least at first, but John slowly developed a keen analytic ability. He did this by reading more carefully, actively participating in class discussions, and by not being satisfied with his initial responses and arguments.

John became skilled at doing this with his readings and textbooks, but he found it much more difficult to critique his professors. Wasn't that being disrespectful? And wouldn't his professors penalize him if he questioned them? What John quickly learned was that professors are human, just like students. Most of them recognized and rewarded John for his analytic skills and encouraged him to challenge their ideas. But there were also those who drew the line of critical thinking at the texts. And John learned, too, that there was a respectful manner in which he could challenge an idea but not the person expressing it. He liked that.

24   Find Yourself a Mentor

We all benefit from good mentoring. You may have had the good fortune of finding a mentor as a teenager, but more than likely finding a mentor in college will be the first occasion for you to have this special relationship. You should give considerable thought to the idea of mentoring, because you will do well to have mentors throughout your life.

Mentors are people who take an interest in you, as a coach, advisor, and supporter for your professional (and sometimes, personal) well-being. The best mentoring relationships come about through a special relationship that develops between the mentor and mentee. Mentors on occasion may have a personal stake in your professional success, but they most often are simply looking out for your best interests, without any self-interest involved. Mentors differ from parents, advisors, friends, teachers, and counselors, though each of those categories of people may at moments overlap and play roles similar to those of mentors. Mentors fall into a unique category all their own.

When a mentor gives you advice, he or she will first and foremost know what your interests and strengths are and will always tailor the discussion very specifically to your individual needs, guiding you away from problem teachers and giving you tips on how to get into the most popular classes even when they are filled.

Mentors can give you the key to open locked doors. They will let you know when there is a great opportunity for an internship or when special speakers are coming to campus. They will strategize with you when you face obstacles. They will listen to you when you are confused and thwarted. They will give you words of uplift and strength when you are feeling down, and they will help you figure out how to chart your course when you are ready to blaze new paths. Mentors truly care about the well-being and success of their mentees.

Formal mentor programs are a good start for learning about the mentoring relationship. They offer you well-meaning people who will take on the characteristics of a mentor in a formalistic role. At the same time, however, an assigned, formal mentor will rarely support and coach you with the passion and commitment of a mutually developed mentor relationship.

You have to take the initiative and responsibility to look for a mentor. The first step is to know that having a mentor is a good idea. The second step is to realize that a good mentoring relationship, like all good relationships, takes time to develop and requires continuing nurturance. Be patient and do not be demanding.

What you can do is try to develop relationships with people you respect and connect with at college. It's often as easy as following up on a professor's comment of interest or praise about a paper you've written or a comment you've made in class. It can mean something as simple as visiting a professor's office hours to talk without having a very specific question or problem to present. Or, it could mean going to a professor or staff person on campus when you do indeed have a problem and taking a risk to trust someone with your personal story.

Good mentors will want time to get to know you, to determine whether they respect you as a person and as a professional. They will want to see the special spark of inner integrity and values that they admire. They will expect that you will be willing to share something about yourself. They will want to know that this will be a relationship that will continue over time. Mentoring relationships are ones of mutual respect and admiration. They involve generosity and giving.

25 Be Both a Thinker and an Activist

Make a commitment to yourself to be a thinking person who will make a difference in the world.

Be a thoughtful agent for social change and social justice, regardless of your political perspective. Develop a passion for involvement and participation that is based on the analytical tools, complex thinking skills, and knowledge learned in your classes.

It's not enough to be just a good thinker or just an activist. You need to be both. You need to learn to apply your thoughtfulness into good practice.

Colleges have a long history of youthful activism. That history is to be celebrated because a democratic society needs dedicated, involved, caring people who are passionate about the pressing issues in their society.

At the same time, that history of activism has also been marked on occasion more by action than by thoughtful analysis. This society and the world at large have little need for stone-throwing students, riots over sporting victories, or yet more simplistic solutions to the complex problems facing the globe.

An increasing number of today's student activists have been trained by well-organized national, governmental, and global agencies to advocate on campus for particular viewpoints. I find this to be a very disappointing trend because these students, however well-meaning, are merely repeating slogans and reproducing documents fed to them by high-priced marketing professionals. What they are doing is the opposite of independent and critical thinking.

You need to be a student who thinks for yourself. Listen to others' points of views, attend lectures, conferences, and information sessions, and read voraciously, but don't become just another ideologue. Your ability to think independently and to bring nuanced, critical reasoning to enormously complex problems is precisely what the world is hoping you will learn to do with your college education. Don't go the simplistic, sound-bite, PR-managed, propaganda route.

Don't assume there is only one right position or room for a debate between just two parties. There may be multiple truths to consider and multiple voices that need to be heard. Where it appears that no solution is to be found or that no one is standing up for what you believe, then take responsibility for finding that solution and standing up for yourself.

Society needs your thoughtful, well-researched, and considered perspective on all matters of public interest. Be sure you speak up so we can all learn from you and make this world a better place for everyone to live in.

26 Pay Attention at Orientation

You've probably been fed so many rules and instructions in your life that you can scarcely imagine that there might be any new ones you've never read. Use a #2 pencil, fill out the bubbles entirely on the standardized test, mark the answer on your chemistry exam with an X, turn in your graduation picture by the following date, use only certain margins on your research papers—you've heard it all over and over again.

I sympathize with your plight. But as you enter college, where you're considered an adult and where your decisions about courses matter and your signatures for tuition payments, housing leases, and various purchases really do have significant associated costs, now would be a really good time to start reading the instructions. And, by the way, since you've been accepted into college, no one is very patient with students who say they haven't read the rules. They know you can read!

After you've made your choice about which college to attend is a very good time to start looking more closely at the mail that comes to you. For months you've probably been immediately throwing out all the catalogs and form letters from all kinds of colleges, some you've never even heard of and some you probably should have applied to. But now the mail that comes is important. Be sure to send in your enrollment deposit, sign up for an orientation date, complete all your financial aid forms, return your housing lease, purchase your football tickets, and note on your calendar when you can move into your residence hall.

At orientation, you should read even more carefully. You're going to take a lot of placement tests. Be sure you fill out the answer sheets properly. Next, read the course bulletin. To be sure, it's boring. But it also serves as the college's academic contract with you. It will tell you what general education/distribution courses are required for you to graduate. It will provide you with the university calendar, so you will know when you have a fall break and when final exams and winter break are held. It will include campus maps, which, as hard as they may be to read, will come in handy on the first day of class when you're lost and need to get to a class in a big hurry.

Next, read the course guide and time schedule. Read about all the courses that are open to you, which have prerequisites and which don't, how many credits you need to complete each term, when and how often courses meet, and when final exams will be held. Check out the rules about dropping and adding classes with or without penalties, about withdrawing from school, about when tuition payments are due.

Reading instructions would certainly rank low on the list of the most intellectually liberating and stimulating tasks in college, but it will surely help you get through the logistics and bureaucracy of college life. And, that's by no means an insignificant task, so don't fight it. Read the rules, figure out the rules, learn all the angles and exceptions to the rules so you know how to use them to benefit your educational experience, and then get on with the good stuff and start having some fun learning.

27 Return to the Three Rs—Reading, 'Riting, and 'Rithmetic

Now that you've been admitted to college, you may be feeling both very confident in your academic abilities and at the same time embarrassed that you still need help with some of the basic foundational learning skills. I find that far too many students, both those from weak high schools as well as those from high schools considered in the top 10 in the country, still need some instruction and support in one or more areas of the "basics." Be sure to get this additional instruction and support.

Even more distressing than the fact that too many students have inadequate skills in the basics is that there is shame associated with it. Students far too often will try to hide their lacking skills in these areas, and faculty far too often do not challenge students to get the instructional support they need.

You can learn all of these skills. And, because you are in college, almost all of which have numerous kinds of academic resource centers and support services, you have an absolutely unique opportunity to learn these skills and get good control of them. Don't try to use your smarts to hide your inadequate high school training: Get assistance! After you graduate from college, you will never have the chance or inclination to go back to these areas of inadequate skills. And, if you feel bad enough now to hide these skill problems, you will feel that much worse after college. Now is the time!!

Why haven't you learned these skills? In some cases, even though you are a very bright person and outstanding student, your K–12 schools have been inadequate and have not provided the basic foundational needs you require in a whole range of areas. In other cases, educational policy in some well-intentioned schools has probably tipped too far to emphasize broader themes of learning and the basic skills have not received sufficient emphasis.

My advice to all of you who find yourself in this situation is to drop any low self-image or embarrassment for needing help with this. This is not a test of your intellectual ability—these are skills! Give yourself an emotional break with this.

Go online or talk to your advisor, your professor, or your friends and find out where the academic resource center is located. Set up a first appointment and plan on coming back for an entire semester. More than likely it will take some time to fully learn these skills.

Finally, go on with your life and enjoy! Know that you're going to do great work in college and beyond.

⟡

LASHONDA WILLIAMS—*"Make a Difference in the World!"*

LaShonda Williams had devoted herself to her community before coming to college. Through programs at her church and through the National Honor Society at high school, she spent many hours each week tutoring children, caring for the elderly, and volunteering at the hospital's cancer ward.

LaShonda's professional dream was to become a doctor, and she was determined to stay on that path during college. LaShonda met with a premed academic advisor during orientation and enrolled in chemistry and calculus for the premed path in addition to her other liberal arts distribution requirements.

When the semester started, LaShonda decided not to pursue extracurricular activities because she knew she would need all the time she had for studying. Even though she had already completed calculus and chemistry in high school, she didn't feel confident enough to jump to the second level of college courses in these disciplines. As a result, the first few weeks of school were mostly review and not too difficult for her. Still, LaShonda studied hard each night, completed all her homework problems and received an A on her first exam.

As the semester progressed, the workload seemed to grow heavier and heavier, and the level of difficulty also increased. LaShonda was pleased that she hadn't gotten involved in extracurricular activities this first term. She saw that she was right that she needed all her time for studying.

LaShonda's friends and the girls on her hall often stopped by to ask her to join them to go to concerts or movies, but LaShonda always declined. As time went on, however, what surprised LaShonda was that it seemed the more time she spent studying, the less she was able to remember, and her homework quality was suffering as well.

LaShonda was disappointed and distressed to find that her grades were beginning to slip. She stayed up later and later each night to study, but it didn't seem to help. She met with her teachers, but that didn't seem to make a difference either. She began to wonder whether she was competitive with other students in the premed track.

LaShonda's friends couldn't help but notice how stressed she was. Her high school friends commented that she wasn't fun to be with anymore. Her new friends at college—well, she didn't really have many new friends because she had been so busy studying that she hadn't met many people.

One day, LaShonda's resident advisor (RA) knocked on her door and invited her to join some others who were going to the hospital to visit and hold sick infants. LaShonda liked her RA and didn't want to say no to her. She went along, reluctantly but felt very guilty that she was not studying.

At the hospital, LaShonda seemed like an entirely different person. As soon as the group arrived in the newborn ward, LaShonda's mood changed. She relaxed, smiled, and was much more sociable with the students she'd gone with. Given all of her experience from high school, she was, of course, very comfortable with the infants and the hospital setting, much more so than many of her peers. Mostly, though, LaShonda was distracted from her chemistry and math homework, and it made her seem like a new person.

On the way back to the residence hall, some of the other students were talking about their classes, and it turned out a couple were in LaShonda's chemistry class. They were complaining vociferously about the teacher and the low grades everyone had been receiving. LaShonda hadn't even been aware that there was a controversy about the teacher or that she wasn't the only one whose grades were falling.

The students just happened to mention they were in a study group, and when they heard LaShonda was studying by herself, they invited her to join their group. "Please come, LaShonda. It's not a big deal," one said. "It's a pretty loose group, but it sure helps me understand the work better when we work out the homework problems together."

When LaShonda sat down that night to finish her homework, she thought a lot about her day. She realized how much she had missed doing community service. Giving back to the community was how she had always defined herself. It had felt so good to hold those babies, and she remembered how much she wanted to make a difference to her community as a doctor.

LaShonda also recognized how much she had missed being a social person. It was downright fun hanging out with the other students, and it had been far too long since she had had some fun at college. She also saw clearly that there was real benefit to be had by studying and commiserating with others. She had been feeling isolated and discouraged, keeping everything to herself, and it was wonderful to share her experiences with other students and to hear from them that they were feeling much the same.

Chemistry and math certainly didn't get any easier that semester. However, with her new friends, LaShonda was much more mentally and emotionally prepared to cope. LaShonda continued to go to the hospital to hold the newborns and became a regular in the study group. She found herself studying just as much as before, but she was more involved socially. She was a much happier and more fulfilled person, and her study time was much more productive. Best of all, she quickly regained confidence in herself and in the fact that she was on the right track, and that medicine was the perfect field of study for her.

28 Manage Your Time Effectively

One of the most important skills you absolutely need to develop is time management. Why? Because college presents you with so much free and unstructured time that unless you know how to organize your day, you will easily and quickly get lost. It may seem like a paradox. How can it be that the more time you have, the more likely you are to find yourself running out of time?

The answer lies in the fact that most new college students have had much of the first eighteen years of their lives very structured. The arrival of college changes all that. Instead of six or seven classes that meet each day, you will probably only be taking about four classes that meet but a few times per week. Instead of having a host of after-school activities or work scheduled each day, you will have significant gaps of free time every day and throughout the day. Instead of a parent making sure you get up and go off to school in the morning or telling you to go to bed at a reasonable hour, your only reminders about going to class or going to sleep will come from yourself or your alarm clock.

So how do you go about managing your time? The first step is to make a schedule—for each day, each week, and each month. Then you need to write the times of all your commitments, including classes, jobs, and any appointments. In the first year of college, it's also not a bad idea to write in mealtimes, because some students get so lost in their free time that they forget about meals or get too busy to find time to eat.

You should now fill in the unstructured time with estimates for study time, recreation, sleep, extracurricular activities, social functions, and even just hanging out. Be sure to fill blocks of time for both study and socializing. You will need both, and you will need limits on both so that you remain a well-rounded person.

Only you will know—and it may even take you some time to discover—how your plans work best in terms of effective study and social time. Do you need to study in short blocks so that an hour between class becomes a powerful study time when you can get a great amount accomplished? Or do you require three- to four-hour-long uninterrupted blocks of time to really focus on a topic. Maybe you need some of both to account for different kinds of assignments.

When you've been studying hard throughout the day, you'll feel good knowing that you've blocked off time on your schedule to go to a campus organization you want to explore, go for a run, or hang out on the hallway with friends.

Before you know it, your days will be filled beyond belief. You will be calling home and telling your parents that you're too busy to talk, that college assignments and expectations are greater than you ever imagined and take loads of time, that you're involved in so many exciting activities, and that your friends have come by to go down to the dining hall for dinner. Hopefully, you will have organized your schedule and learned to manage your time so that you are comfortable doing all of these wonderful things. You've learned about your study needs, and you've built a schedule that allocates plenty of time to complete your assignments but also keeps you balanced socially.

29 Participate in Learning Communities and Other Special Academic Programs

How do you make yourself known to others on campus? In your first weeks and months on campus, how do you set yourself apart so that people in your new environment will have a chance to meet the very special and unique person that is you?

One of the best ways to be recognized is to sign yourself up for one of the many special academic programs on campus. Learning communities, mentoring programs, research opportunity programs, and honors programs are all good examples of academic structures that will let people get to know you and allow you to stand out from the rest of the first-year student class.

These and other similar programs give you a chance to meet other students, faculty, and staff on a more personal basis. These programs enable you to get the personal and individualized attention that you deserve as a very bright, new college student.

Some students worry that they don't want to be limited by enrolling in specialized programs. In my experience, it's very rare that colleges set up programs that impose limits. Rather, these are opportunities that help with the initial transition to college, establish smaller communities in which you can build close friendships, and actually open doors to give you easy access to all the rich resources of the wider campus. These programs seek to get you more deeply engaged in campus activities than you would be if you did not participate in them.

Other students are looking for a degree of anonymity when they attend college. My advice, even for these students, is still to join one of these special, individualized programs. You will certainly have more than enough chances at college to blend in with the crowd and not feel constrained by a very small, closed community. And that is the case even in these programs.

Learning communities, perhaps more than any other college offering, emphasize the academic or scholarly community that can exist between faculty and students as part of the college experience. They provide an environment in which you will easily develop friendships with other students. Faculty and staff will get to know you, respect your unique character and potential, and care about you as an individual.

Some learning communities, known as living-learning programs, are residential, meaning that students live together in the same residence hall and take courses with faculty who share a common interest in a particular academic theme. Other, nonresidential learning communities assign the same set of students to two or more classes or link faculty from different fields to team teach a single group of students in a way that creates intellectual connections between the different subjects.

Mentoring programs assign faculty, staff, or upper-class students to an individual student or to groups of students to provide advice and support. Sometimes these mentors will take students to lunch or to a campus concert or invite them home for dinner and conversation.

Research opportunity programs give students a chance to work closely with a faculty member, a graduate research assistant, and perhaps a few other undergraduates on the faculty member's research project. It's another avenue for building a relationship with faculty and students through an academic endeavor.

Honors programs generally invite a select group of students to their programs based on high school grades and standardized test scores and provide these students with greater academic challenges or recognition to take some courses together.

You should definitely look into one of these special academic programs. They will help ensure that you continue to be recognized in college for your unique talents as a student and as an individual. They will also enable you to take advantage of the very best educational experiences that colleges have to offer.

30 Visit Your Academic Advisor Often

Think of your academic advisor as your coach. A coach's goal is to help you grow, improve your skills, prepare you for each upcoming challenge, and achieve your goals.

In college, the academic advisor's primary purpose is to help you succeed in your academic work. Their service and advice are free. You can visit as often as you want. At most colleges you can even change your academic advisor if you don't hit it off with an assigned advisor or if you don't believe that person is the right fit for you. What more could you ask for?

Like a coach, the academic advisor not only is looking out for you but is responsible for following the institutional rules. Your advisor will work with you to keep track of the requirements you have completed and those you still need to complete. Your advisor will want to talk with you if your grades are slipping or if you are in academic trouble.

Because some students view the academic advisor in this role as the gatekeeper and rule enforcer or as the person who intervenes only when academic difficulties arise, they maintain some distance from the advising office. That is a mistake. Remember, like coaches, academic advisors want students to succeed academically and graduate from college. Their goal is not to make problems for you.

Your advisor can give you tips on good classes to take. Advisors constantly hear from students about the quality and rigor of various courses and different faculty. They are tremendous resources. Ask them lots of questions to get the information that you feel you need to know.

What advisors like best is to think together with you about your intellectual interests, professional goals, and life commitments. They want to help you chart your own path but want you to make the decisions about what course to take or path to choose. They see themselves as facilitators. They want you to do the necessary work of identifying and clarifying your own individual desires and goals.

It's your college education, and you get to make the choices. Colleges provide you with a great resource in the form of academic advisors. They know a great deal of information that will help you make your way, and they are at your service free of charge, as often as you'd like. If academic advisors didn't exist at college, you would want to invent the idea or find someone to hire to do this very same job on your behalf. They're that valuable. Be sure to take advantage of this great resource!

Faculty and Classes

31 Choose Good Teachers over Good Class Topics

Always choose the best teacher when you are planning your class schedule for the next semester. Course topics and descriptions will catch your attention, especially in college, when you will have hundreds or even thousands of courses to choose from each semester. Course topics are without a doubt important; however, a good teacher will always trump a good course title or description.

A good teacher will make any topic interesting and any course a worthwhile experience for you. You can get information and read about any topic or idea throughout your life. But a good teacher—or especially a great teacher—is a rare find, and you want to take full advantage of such an opportunity.

Good teachers force you to think and learn. They will be demanding of you, but they will be even more demanding of themselves. They will expect you to contribute to the success of the class and come to class prepared each day. They will be available and accessible to you, and they will be interested in what you are learning from the class.

Good teachers can be entertaining, but that's only occasionally the case. In fact, you should make a careful distinction between those faculty who stand out as good entertainers and those who are good teachers. Sometimes you may want to sit back in lectures and be entertained, or you may want to balance a course load with either heavy quantitative/lab or reading/writing assignments with one from another other category. Good teachers will certainly help make learning interesting, stimulating, and enjoyable, but they may not be entertainers, and they will very likely require you to work and think very hard.

When you enroll in a course whose topic you like and whose description sounds interesting, you are likely to find it to be a great learning experience. But savvy students talk with peers, older students, advisors, and even other faculty to find out more about who is teaching such an interesting topic. Some colleges post teaching evaluations of faculty and courses on student government Web sites. Some larger introductory courses on topics such as chemistry, statistics, psychology, and history are taught every semester by different faculty, so it makes perfect sense to wait a semester or two until you can take the subject with the best instructor.

With good teachers, you will learn new content areas, you will be challenged to think deeply, and you will be asked to examine issues analytically and from multiple perspectives. You will be expected to do your best work, and you will want to do just that because of the high standards that the professors hold for you and for themselves. You should take this opportunity to meet these professors through classroom interactions and at office hours and get to know them throughout the semester.

If you enroll in a class with a good faculty member teaching a course topic you're interested in, then you've hit the jackpot! Even for just that single course, you're going to have a terrific semester! Count on it!

32 Pursue Your Intellectual Passions

Do you love to read historical novels? Could you spend hours conceptualizing and then tinkering with the mechanics of a science project? Do you write poetry or do graphic arts in your free time? Are you consumed with the environmental crisis that global warming represents? Do you love to look at rock formations? Are you fascinated by the intersection of economics, international conflict, and ethnic hatred?

Dig deep into your life history to come up with a list of subjects that you've found fascinating, troubling, exciting, and just plain worth your time to think about. Begin to identify what you really care about and then find a way to pursue or at least explore these subject areas in college.

Many students, even those who are liberal arts students, imagine that there are significant constraints on their course selections. First, they are under the impression that they must immediately complete all of their distribution or general education requirements. Second, they feel considerable pressure to take a prescribed set of courses that they believe are required to advance them toward particular majors and preprofessional degrees. Students interested in business, for instance, feel pressured to major in economics. Students interested in law feel pressured to major in political science.

In truth, most students actually have a much greater degree of flexibility for course electives than they imagine when they first enter college. Yes, you do need to pay attention to general education or distribution requirements at your college, and you should draft a plan of how you anticipate fulfilling all or many of those requirements during the first two years. But you have room for electives! Professional programs are much more open to applicants with a broad set of interests than most students imagine. Many law schools would love to have a few more philosophy majors.

I urge you to think of your personal list of favorite subjects—your passions and interests—as another set of requirements that you fulfill during college, with equal standing to all the other requirements. You must effectively advocate for your personal set of requirements, your passions and interests, and negotiate the other general education, major, and preprofessional requirements to create a balance in your course schedule and in your life. Be a strong advocate for your own set of favored requirements because this negotiation will be one of the decisive factors in determining whether you feel satisfied with your college education.

Remember, this is *your* college education, and you only get one chance at it! You need to be true to yourself. This is the time in your life to explore those topics that excite you and to pursue those dreams that drive your intellectual passions.

33 Make Intellectual Connections among Courses

It may not count for a grade, but some of your best learning will take place when you take time to bring intellectual coherence to the wide range of courses you take each semester and each year.

A growing number of colleges are attempting to create opportunities for you to make the linkages among the seemingly disparate courses you take from the different disciplines, where you get only a sociological or biological or literary perspective. Learning communities and senior capstone courses are newer curricular efforts at many colleges to bring the importance of cross-disciplinary perspectives to bear on particular issues and topics. If your college offers these innovative programs, you should take advantage of them. If these programs are not offered, you should still try to make these linkages.

The idea is simple enough. As scholars study the complex issues of their fields and of society, it makes sense that they would want to bring to bear the full power of the intellectual perspectives and understandings of thinkers from all disciplines and departments in higher education. The same would be true in your courses. However, our colleges and universities are organized into departments according to their disciplines. Unfortunately, professors from one department commonly don't interact very frequently with their colleagues from the next department.

If you are studying environmental issues, you will need to know not only the science of the environment but also the social, political, economic, and humanistic understandings of the environment. If each of your courses focuses on just one discrete aspect of the environment, then it will be up to you to integrate the perspectives of all these fields as you attempt to better understand environmental issues. If you look at the environment only from the perspective of a biologist or an economist, you will be missing the full picture needed to make informed analyses.

If you intend to focus on the health sciences, the same is true. To better understand problems related to sexually transmitted diseases, you will want to take a wide variety of courses in genetics and the sciences, education, economics, sociology, and literature, among others. However, you will also want to do the work of making connections among what you have learned in each of these courses. Without doing so, you may become an expert in one particular area of your field, but your expertise will be narrowly tailored and limited in its impact.

This intellectual work not only will benefit your intellectual understanding of your particular field but will help to broaden your skills in doing broad multidisciplinary thinking across fields. You want to strengthen your critical thinking skills, broaden your horizons, and, at the same time, focus on a particular disciplinary area by the time you graduate. Too many students find themselves graduating with some breadth and some depth and very few if any connections among things they've learned.

Make this one of your challenges in college. Know that you can be all of these—deep, broad, analytical, and able to connect the dots across disciplinary subject fields and course topics.

ANGELA NELSON—*"You Mean I Can Take a Class That I'm Interested In?"*

Angela Nelson arrived at orientation with few expectations. She knew how to do well in school, but she had never been excited by any of her high school classes. Angela was aware that there were lots of requirements in college, and anticipated taking the usual load of English, history, math, science and Spanish, just as she had in high school.

It wasn't that Angela didn't have any academic interests. She loved history, but she was so tired of all those years of U.S. history. She had enjoyed science till she started her AP classes, which took so much time and always seemed more focused on what she referred to as "that stupid AP test," than on anyone learning anything interesting about science. She had liked math in middle school but was pretty much burned out from all the hours she had put in doing problem sets during high school. Spanish? Well, she was so frustrated with the attitude of her Spanish teachers in high school that sometimes she wished she had taken another language.

At summer orientation Angela met with her academic advisor, Tom, who in-

sisted she call him by his first name. His first question was, "So, what subjects interest you, Angela?" Angela was sure this question would be shortly followed by a "Well, that's very nice, but you'll have to wait till your junior year till you can take those courses because first you'll have to fill all your requirements." Surprisingly, though, Tom said the exact opposite. He actually encouraged Angela to take the very courses about which she was most excited. She was shocked! "When is the 'sorry, but' coming in this scenario?" she thought to herself.

Angela found a Middle Eastern history course she was really interested in and an English course that focused on women's literature. She loved the idea of taking a psychology class, but her advisor recommended instead that she do an independent research project—for credit—with a very popular psychology professor. That sounded so great! And she decided to take an environmental science class that was project-based, focusing on the health of the river that flowed along the campus outskirts.

Tom sensed her enthusiasm and suggested that they brainstorm a list of courses and projects that she might take over the next couple of years. First, Angela listed study abroad as a priority because she wanted to use the Spanish she had studied all these years, but she wondered if she could manage going abroad for a year and still fulfill all her requirements. Angela learned that there were all kinds of study abroad opportunities. She could study abroad for a year, for a semester, or just for a summer. There were intensive language programs that lasted just one month. And her college even offered research projects organized by individual professors that lasted two to four weeks and took place abroad.

Angela had always wanted to take art history and music appreciation. She also had thought about journalism as a possible profession, and her advisor suggested that she first try writing for the school newspaper to see if she liked the field. That sounded so exciting, and apparently the newspaper accepted first year students as reporters. Some other science classes also sounded very interesting to her, with real-world foci on topics like AIDS, sexuality, and genetics.

Angela walked out of Tom's office so thrilled she had to pinch herself to make sure she wasn't dreaming. "I'm free!" she exclaimed to no one in particular. "This is so different from high school. I can't wait to start my classes."

34 Go to Office Hours and Get to Know Your Instructors

It is so important for you to visit your professors during office hours.

Some students are wary about going to office hours. You've been told so many stories through the admissions process about how renowned and prestigious your college's faculty are that you may feel intimidated about having a one-on-one discussion with your professor. You might be wondering why your professors would want to spend their time talking with you, a first-year student, when they have books to read, lectures to prepare, articles to write, research to complete, and other colleagues to talk with.

Most students come to office hours right after an exam to complain about their grades or to get help with what when wrong. Those are reasonable things to talk about with your professor, and you should definitely ask about what you didn't understand in an exam. However, as a general rule, they're the least interesting topics for the professor, and if that's the only time you visit, they're not likely to lead to building a stronger relationship. Other students come to the professor just prior to an upcoming exam or paper. That's also a good reason to speak with your professor. The only difficulty may be that if you come just before the assignment due date, then you're likely to be rushed through your meeting because you'll be waiting in line with lots of your classmates. Once again, this is another good reason to see the professor, but it won't likely be a relationship builder.

The best time to visit office hours is during those times in the semester when there is no imminent paper or exam. You should just stop by, and be prepared to ask and talk about one of the course readings or topics. If you have some background on the topic, share that with the professor. You might also want to ask the professor about his or her broader interest and experience in the field. Find out more about what professors do in their lives, what their interests are, and what projects they're currently working on.

You'll likely find that your professor will help guide this discussion and will take an interest in you. Even if it doesn't seem that way at first, you might be surprised one day when the professor stops you on the way out of class and follows up on your earlier conversation. Yes, she was really listening! If you go back to the professor's office that next week or the week after, you're likely to have twice the impact and twice the possibility of building an ongoing relationship.

You need to think of your professor's turf as your turf: the entire college is your academic learning environment, and as a member of the scholarly community, you have a right and a responsibility to feel at home in all the academic departments where you are taking classes. Faculty hold office hours precisely to meet with students in their classes; it's not the time they set aside to do research or other intellectual work. If you don't come to see your professor during office hours, he or she will still be sitting in the office but all alone during that time.

All faculty were college students themselves, and part of what they appreciate about their lives as professors is the opportunity to engage with interested and interesting students, just like you.

35 Become Skilled at Different Ways of Knowing

As a result of your many years of schooling, you have become an expert learner—or at least you are expert in some ways of learning. College offers you the opportunity to learn in many different ways. You would do well to explore these different paths to knowledge, to gain some experience with all of them, and to identify which approaches are best suited to your learning style.

Not everyone learns in the same way. Some of your peers find sheer joy in solving mathematical problems. Others love to spend hours in the lab working on chemical experiments. A sophomore student of mine recently told me that in third grade, when the other kids were playing ball at recess, she was busy writing, developing, and handing out questionnaires on all sorts of topics. What means of learning is most stimulating to you?

In college, you will find yourself in small discussion groups and in large lectures. There are benefits to both. Learn how to be an active participant in discussions and to get the most out of listening to lectures by learned scholars.

In addition to these more traditional means, some students find that they love to learn through experiential approaches. Experiential learning might mean working in an urban high school as you study about education, children, or the life of cities. It could mean designing a new traffic system as part of an engineering class. You might work in city hall on developing a new budget as part of a public policy course. Critical to experiential learning is that you take time for study and reflection about your experiences.

What are other approaches to learning that you should explore? These approaches might include discovery and exploration through research, writing a thesis, collaborative or individual projects, disciplinary study as well as interdisciplinary study.

High schools often emphasize one learning approach over others, and different groups of students may have been encouraged to develop their skills in certain methods and fields. For instance, men and women have traditionally had different experience with levels of encouragement in math; the same is true of white students and students of color. Regardless of your high school preparation, you should strive to gain good skills in all these areas.

Finally, you should become serious about the learning opportunities you will find outside as well as inside the classroom. Lectures, poetry readings, art exhibits, musical concerts, and theater are great learning opportunities. Participating in or becoming a leader of an organization will provide you with skills, insights, and experiences that you cannot learn through lectures or books. Internships, community service projects, acting in a play, writing for the school newspaper, producing a campus show, even working in the residence hall cafeteria or in an academic department's office are all wonderfully rich learning opportunities that you should consider.

36 Take Small Classes and Seminars

The seminar class is the epitome of the college experience. It is what college is all about. There you are, with ten to twenty other intellectually curious students, exploring new ideas and perspectives with a college professor. You raise questions, voice opinions, present critical insights, and listen to the ideas and analyses of your peers and your professor. People in the room challenge each other to think more critically and explore the topic in greater depth.

Your professor guides you beyond surface understandings and interpretations to new and more complex understandings of the day's topic. You realize that your intellectual capacity is so much greater than you ever imagined. You are intellectually invigorated, and you and your classmates carry the class discussion into your thoughts and conversations throughout the day, continuing the conversation as you walk across campus after class.

In a small class you participate as an active learner. Your voice counts and will be heard. You will have the chance to present ideas, discuss readings, and engage with your teacher and fellow students in lively discourse. You will learn how to engage with others who hold different viewpoints. You will learn the important difference between the competitive debate model of discussion and the more collaborative form, intellectual inquiry.

The success of a small class depends as much on the quality of student participation as on the professor's teaching qualities. Unlike most classes you've probably taken before, you carry a significant share of responsibility for class dynamics, the vibrancy of discussion, and the level of analytical thinking that takes place. When you do your work and come prepared to class, your peers and teacher all learn more deeply that class session. You make a difference in the classroom.

Another important advantage of small classes is that you will have a chance to get to know a faculty member in a close and personal way. You will get a good insight on how faculty think and how they approach intellectual issues. You will develop a special relationship with this one particular professor because of the regular, ongoing contact.

In addition to getting to know a faculty member, the seminar also provides you with a unique opportunity to get to know your fellow college students. From your seminar conversations, you will learn about how each one thinks and how each one sees the world from a unique and special perspective. You will build close relationships with some of your classmates precisely because of your common classroom experience and the active, in-depth and sometimes intense discussions.

Whether you are in a large public university or a small private college, you will have opportunities to take both large and small classes. Both types of courses certainly have value, but be sure to enroll in as many small classes or seminars as you can.

37 Participate in Undergraduate Research Programs

One of the best learning opportunities available to you in college is to participate directly in one of the central activities of higher education, the exploration and discovery of new ideas, new perspectives, and new knowledge. By working with faculty on their research projects, even as a first-year student, you will develop essential research skills and gain a unique insight into the world of research.

Your professors are always involved in new and ongoing research projects. Some of this research takes place in science labs, doing basic research that may eventually lead to health-related discoveries, for example. Some do computer modeling for scientific research, engineering, public policy, and economic forecasting. Other faculty conduct surveys in local communities, in hospitals, via mail or the Internet, on a national or international basis. Still other faculty do archival research in libraries, while others immerse themselves in communities to interview and observe how people live and think and to better understand the cultures of which they are a part.

Joining a research project has many benefits. First, at many colleges today, established programs will offer you course credit or work-study payment for your participation. Every student learns basic research skills in the field of the project on which they are working. Given the right circumstances, the right project, and the right set of skills, some students will have an opportunity to work with others to coauthor a research paper or to present research findings at a conference. Imagine, in your first or second year of college, having the university pay for you to travel to a conference to present your own research! You also will have a chance to get to know a faculty member and often graduate students as well, in their academic domain.

Here is how these programs often work. You must apply to undergraduate research programs. Some schools may limit participation to honors students, but this opportunity will more likely be open to any motivated student. Faculty who have volunteered to utilize undergraduates in their research will fill out information sheets about their projects, which you can then review to decide which holds greatest interest for you. You will then go interview with your top choices, and then one of the faculty, or hopefully more than one, will make you an offer to join the project.

Enjoy this wonderful learning opportunity as a young researcher!

38 Take a Course Pass/Fail

The pass/fail option gives you the freedom to learn unburdened by grades. Imagine that! Your learning takes precedence—it, rather than the grade that usually follows, is the prize, the reward, and the centerpiece of your work in the course.

A pass/fail course allows you to focus on what you learn in a course without the pressure and interference of a grade. It also provides you with an opportunity to experiment in your course selection by taking any course, but usually one out of your field, that you think will be particularly challenging without having to be overly concerned about getting a lower grade.

Like it or not, too much of your time and attention will likely be spent worrying about what grades you will receive in your classes. Your purpose at college is to learn. Yet our education system, to a deleterious extent, has tried to equate grades with learning. They're not the same.

I know too many students who look at the grade on a paper or test and then ignore the professor's extensive comments. Students often ask whether an assignment will be on the test, thinking there is no intrinsic value in the course assignments but only how they will be factored into grades. Faculty-student conversations and office hours are too often downgraded to test preparation and grade appeals/complaints rather than opportunities for learning and participation in the scholarly community.

The pass/fail option allows you to take risks in your course selection. A nonscience major who is interested in chemistry but worries that she might get a low grade competing with premed students can take the course pass/fail and just drop all the worries. A student studying

Spanish for his or her second language requirement might want to take a semester of Chinese but worries about ruining an otherwise high grade point average. Taking the class pass/fail may be just the answer.

If your college offers the pass/fail option, definitely use it, and use it wisely. Learning for the purpose of learning, without the mediating presence of a grade, is likely to be a liberating educational experience. You will quickly appreciate what people mean when they speak of the love of learning.

39 Consider an Independent Study Course

An independent study is a unique opportunity to design a course based on your specific interests and to study individually with a professor.

You may have an interest in a particular subject area that is not offered in the college curriculum or that does not receive the intense focus that you desire. You might be intrigued by a course on modern U.S. history and then wish to study in depth the role of U.S. presidents during times of war. You might take a required course on diversity and then want to study the civil rights movement in depth. After taking a comparative literature course, you might want to read all the works of a particular author.

An independent study will allow you the opportunity to design your own course syllabus to focus on the exact subject matter in which you are most interested. An independent study also allows you to work in the manner that best suits you. You might prefer to write a lengthy research paper or many short essays rather than to take any exams. You might love to read and so might choose to design an independent study in which you read far more extensively than a typical course would allow you because of all the papers and exams assigned. You might want to learn experientially but be studying in a department that doesn't offer experiential courses in your field.

To get permission to do an independent study, there are a few prerequisites. First, you must be a highly self-motivated and organized individual. You will need to design the course and the requirements (with input and approval from the faculty member), and do all the work with minimal oversight. Typically, you will meet with your faculty member fewer than a half dozen times per semester. Second, you must have a burning interest in a topic that is not offered elsewhere on campus. Third, you must know a faculty member who thinks very highly of you, who has an interest in the subject matter you propose, and who is willing to give up his or her time to sponsor and oversee your study.

Faculty who sponsor independent studies do so out of the goodness of their hearts and out of their commitment to supporting student learning. They get no credit from their departments for helping you out. They are willing to give their time for your intellectual benefit. Therefore, you want to be sure you follow through on every aspect of your independent study, make your meetings with the professor intellectually interesting to both of you, and make the entire process as smooth and easy as possible for the faculty member.

If you are a motivated student, the independent study will give you the opportunity to get credit for learning in the manner you know best, about a topic you have the greatest interest, and with a faculty member you respect, whom you want to learn from, and with whom you want to strengthen your relationship.

40 Go to Class on Time (and Other Rules of the Classroom)

There is an assumption in college that you have made a deliberate and intentional decision to enter the scholarly community of higher education and that you have accepted the responsibilities that are a part of that community. This means that there is an expectation that you will behave in a respectful manner to your professors and peers and that they will be respectful toward you.

One of the delights of the college classroom, in comparison to K–12 classes, is that there are relatively few discipline problems. Students know they are in college to learn. They are there by choice, not by parental or state law, and, for the most part, they act like adult learners.

The first sign of respect is to go to class and to go on time. Particularly in a small class, you are responsible for contributing to the course's success. You cannot contribute if you do not attend. Whether you are in a small or large class, when you come to class late, you disrupt and interrupt the lecture or discussion that is in progress.

Turn off your cell phone. It's rude to everyone around for you to receive phone calls during class. Further, if you answer your phone in the middle of class and proceed to have a conversation, know that your behavior is disrespectful and unacceptable.

Don't read the newspaper during class. Would you like someone to read the paper when you were discussing an idea with them? During class, don't play games or read e-mail on your computer while pretending to take notes. You might wonder if this behavior happens only as a result of a particularly boring professor, but I have seen students routinely read papers and work on crossword puzzles even during other students' presentations. Please don't allow yourself to adopt such behavior.

Don't sleep during class. If you are so tired that you can't stay awake, then you shouldn't be in class. No one wants you there when you are sleeping. Go home and go to bed.

Don't whisper to your neighbor in class. I see this behavior mostly from students who went to high school together. That they continue to behave like they were in high school is clear to everyone in the class. If you have something so important and urgent to tell your friend that you must do so during class, then you should leave the classroom, have the conversation elsewhere, and act on the emergency you are facing. Otherwise, don't whisper.

Be a respectful learner and member of the higher education learning community. Think of your class as a community. Get yourself mentally situated to be engaged in the learning process the moment class starts. Come to class prepared. Be ready to ask questions and to offer analyses and insights. Practice good listening skills. Get to know the professor as well as your fellow classmates.

It is a privilege to attend college. I find that first-generation college students are always among the most respectful students in class. They seem to have a special appreciation for the power and privilege that are captured in the opportunity to be part of a scholarly community at an institution of higher learning. They are joined by 98–99% of their classmates in that respectful behavior. Be a member of this respectful majority, and never forget how fortunate you are.

41 Read the Reading Assignments

Reading assignments represent one of the big differences between high school and college. In high school, you were tested on just about anything and everything you were assigned to read. In college, the expectation is that you will want to read everything assigned because the reason you are in college is that you want to learn as much as possible. In some cases you will be tested on reading assignments, but not always. If you are tested, it will be in much more comprehensive and analytic ways.

Professors read everything they can get their hands on. They are constantly trying to get hold of the latest works in their field and beyond. When you enter their classes, especially in the first year of college, they assume—usually accurately—that you are smart and interested in the topic but know very little about the subject they are teaching. They feel compelled to load up the readings so that you can enter into the discussion of the topic. In their minds, some foundational theories, arguments, and texts are essential background information to begin the first class discussions.

You, as a typical student, are wondering if all this reading is going to be tested or if you will need to present it all back in a paper. You are thinking, based on your high school experience, that if the homework is not going to be tested or graded—and certainly if it's not going to be discussed—then there's no need for it to be assigned or for you to read it. Your professor, however, has no interest in listening to you merely repeating back the main points of this introductory material. She wants to move forward quickly to the much more nuanced literature to begin discussions in class of the more complex issues in the field.

In those subjects in which everyone has personal experience, such as family, gender relations, education, and so on, first-year students sometimes complain that the readings are just repeating the same obvious point over and over again. If you find yourself making that complaint, step back for a moment and think about how carefully you are reading the assignments. After all, your professor has spent her entire academic life reading and researching the topic you are now studying. Faculty are asking you to join them as junior colleagues, going beyond the typical surface-level understandings of the topic to the deeper and more complex layers of analysis.

As a college-educated person, you want to understand issues beyond the sound bites you hear on TV news shows or the shouting debates that pit one TV guest versus the next. Those shows give off lots of heat but shed no light and offer no insight. In contrast, the assigned readings and accompanying class discussions will take you beyond the superficial conversations to a different level.

This society needs college-educated thinkers who have the skills and understanding to analyze the most complex and vexing problems facing the world. Do the readings not as an assignment but as an opportunity to become an educated citizen, a well-informed and worldly person, and an analytic thinker. If you read and read deeply, you will begin the process of becoming one of these much needed well-educated citizens.

42 Don't Fall Behind: Learn to Be Both the Tortoise and the Hare

Time will play tricks with your mind at the start of college. You will think that you have loads of free time for studying. You will be surprised in the first weeks of the semester that some professors teaching subjects such as math and chemistry are reviewing material that you already covered in high school. You will take heart that only a few papers are required in any given social science or humanities course over the entire semester.

What's the big deal? you will think. College does not seem as difficult as you always heard about. Instead of studying, you may choose to fill your time with extracurricular activities, clubs, socializing in the residence hall, or watching lots of TV.

Then—and it will seem like it hits all of a sudden—the pace will change dramatically. The first exams will be held. The first set of papers will be due. Instead of review, your professors will begin covering new material two or three times as fast as you ever learned anything in high school. In each class you will be reading entire books in a week and multiple, high-level academic articles for each class session.

How will you keep up when the semester shifts into warp speed? The answer is simple. You will need to have the best traits of both the tortoise and the hare. You need to be steady and consistent in your study habits, ready for the long haul of the semester. At the same time, you need to be ready for the bursts of energy required when there is an especially heavy load of tests or papers any given week. That won't happen often, but it will happen, so it's best to keep yourself in good mental and physical health for those times when you need to set everything aside to get all your work done.

The key is to always keep up with your work, even when the workload seems light. Falling behind and catching up later should not be an option. Trust me on this one—it won't work. By keeping up with your work, you will be in good shape when a rush of assignments from multiple classes are all due at once. It will allow you flexibility for those times when you catch a cold, have heavy extracurricular commitments, or something very exciting comes up spontaneously.

Keep in mind that generations of college students have been able to keep up with the heavy workload. You very clearly have all the intellectual ability and schooling experience not only to keep up but to excel in all your subjects. Just remember to be both the tortoise and the hare, and don't let yourself fall behind.

NEAL PATEL—*"I've Got So Much Free Time!"*

Neal Patel's course schedule was made in heaven. No Friday classes. Mondays and Wednesdays he had class from one o'clock to four o'clock, and Tuesdays and Thursdays he had class from ten to twelve and four to six. Neal figured he could sleep late every day, start his weekend partying on Thursday night, and pretty much play around much of the semester. When he moved into his room at the start of the semester, he spent a lot of time setting up his home theater speaker system to get the best sound imaginable for his music and TV.

Neal started the semester sleeping late and staying up to all hours of the night. He planned to do his homework Sunday afternoons but ended up watching football. Monday and Wednesday mornings were open times for study, but he usually got up too late to get anything useful done. His best study time was between class on Tuesdays and Thursdays, from twelve to four, but in reality it was one to four, because he liked to talk with his friends leisurely over lunch.

Friday afternoon was supposed to be another study time, but he was usually already in the weekend party mode by that time.

Neal was a smart guy, and he thought he could keep up with his studies pretty well. He did the bare minimum, which always did the trick in high school. But he quickly found out that this wouldn't work in college. On his first paper, he got a C− with some pretty harsh comments from his professor. His first chemistry exam resulted in an E.

Neal was already heavily involved in his fraternity rush activities. Since he always seemed to be available, the frat brothers began to call on him to help with parties and other activities during the week and on weekends. Neal loved that he was so popular in the college fraternity and that he could keep up with the best of the hard partiers and drinkers, even those who were juniors and seniors. He often hung out till three in the morning in the frat house, talking and drinking with the guys and doing various chores.

One of Neal's professors contacted him about his grades and told him to come to office hours. Neal was in major denial about his academic work and felt like he didn't have to respond to the professor. But this professor kept after him and insisted he stay after the next class to talk with her. She questioned him about his unsatisfactory work and about his obviously disinterested body language in class. She told him that he would fail the course if his work didn't significantly improve. Neal was slightly embarrassed at this conversation and told her he'd try harder.

Two weeks later he failed another test, this one in Spanish. Neal's Spanish teacher sent him an e-mail requesting to speak with him. Neal was impressed that people were taking an interest in him, but he also felt humiliated, like a little schoolboy being sent to detention. However, this professor, unlike the first, challenged him about his party habits and asked whether he had an alcohol problem. He even asked whether Neal was hoping to fail—maybe he didn't really want to be in college and would prefer to take a year off.

Neal was kind of stunned to be having these conversations with his college professors. That night he called a close friend from home whom he hadn't talked with since the first week of school. He shared what had happened. His friend was understanding but also very honest in expressing his disappointments about Neal's behavior and approach to college. Neal began to wonder what had gone wrong for him.

Neal made a commitment to himself to get back on track. He met with his academic advisor to map out a strategy. To his surprise, even the advisor questioned whether Neal wanted to withdraw from the semester altogether, because it would be so difficult to dig himself out of this hole. His advisor also referred him to a personal counselor, saying that if he were serious about his studies, he would first have to get more serious about getting his life back on track.

In the end, Neal passed his courses that term with a C− average. He worked out a very detailed schedule—day by day, hour by hour—of study time, class time, and some time for fun. He realized that what he had written off as free time in his high school mind-set was really meant to be study time in college. There really was no other way around it. Neal cut way back on his fraternity activities. Some of the brothers were critical and gave him a hard time, but others really supported him in getting his priorities in order. Neal's professors commented on his changed attitude and performance, but it was a major shock to him to get final grades of Cs and Ds instead of As and Bs.

When Neal came home for winter break, he spoke honestly with his parents for the first time and told them that he had done poorly in his first semester of college. Neal's parents were disappointed, angry, and concerned. They offered their support and help, but Neal could tell he had lost some of their respect. Neal said he had learned a lot about the need to find balance in his life.

It took another semester of time management advice and low grades before Neal really did get his priorities in life in order. He realized that he truly hadn't been ready for the demands of college that year. He was certainly smart enough, *but he hadn't been ready for the freedoms he had been given in terms of free time and independence. He may not have gotten good grades that year, but he sure learned a most important lesson that would serve him well throughout his life.*

43 Think Sensibly and Strategically about Grades

How should you think about grades in college? Grades are such an overriding concern for most high school students because of the tremendous pressures to gain admission to the college of their choice. But what happens to grades in college?

Let's first do the mathematics of college grades. The most traditional college plan would have you take an average of four courses each semester, attend two semesters of college each year, and go to college for four years. That comes to thirty-two classes. Thus, the final grade for each class you take counts only about 3% of your final college grade point average. In each class, you will have an average of four assignments/exams that comprise your grade. If each of these assignments were weighted equally, then each would be worth less than 1%, or .75%, of your final college grade point average.

Keep the above calculations in mind when you get your first grades on papers or tests in your first semester of college. If you get your first ever C on your first exam—and many students do get lower-than-expected grades on their first papers and exams—use it as a learning experience about the difference between high school and college expectations for quality of work and the necessity of good study skills. But don't panic about it being a career-ending signal. That C you received counted only

.75% of your final college GPA. It didn't rule you out for a career in medicine, law, or teaching or for doctoral studies in biology or sociology.

Some students vociferously argue about getting an A− grade rather than an A. If you think your professor made a mathematical error or some other clear and legitimate mistake in your grade, bring it to his attention. Otherwise, just forget about it. Relax. An A− grade means you were nearly excellent in your work in that course. Feel good about your accomplishment.

If you think you deserve an A on a paper because your high school teacher praised your writing and your college professor has numerous suggestions on how you can improve, please don't complain. What you need to do, instead, is adjust your expectations and raise your own standards. If you believe you need an A to get into business school, don't think your sense of entitlement will go very far with your professor.

Grades can still be meaningful in college, but their meaning is quite different. On the one hand, if you are applying to certain professional schools, like medicine or law, your GPA along with standardized test scores will certainly be one of the important admissions criteria. On the other hand, if you are applying to graduate programs, while grades are considered, there will be less attention to insignificant grade differentials, such as whether you received a 3.8 or a 3.7 GPA. Faculty letters of reference, special accomplishments in the discipline, and work or research experience in the field will often carry considerable weight in conjunction with the more traditional measures. If you plan to go out and look for a job after you receive your B.A., few employers will look closely or exclusively at your grade point average.

However, there is a marked ranking difference in terms of the value of the degree for students who plan to pursue advanced degrees. Clearly, those who receive a 3.5 GPA or higher are in a far stronger position than those who graduate with a 2.5 GPA or lower. In this sense, grades do matter significantly. But they shouldn't matter to the extent that you focus on grades more than you focus on learning or that you lose any of the joy of the college experience for the achievement of a high grade point average. Further, they shouldn't cause you to worry endlessly about any single low grade you receive.

Many faculty wish they didn't have to grade—they would prefer to give students careful feedback and not just a letter grade, with all the baggage that grades carry. Other faculty do believe it's important to sort out students, particularly in larger introductory classes, in order to give students a realistic assessment of their capabilities for graduate study in certain professional fields. Faculty approaches to grading vary across fields of study, and faculty themselves disagree with one another about issues of grade inflation.

Think about how you want to approach the issue of grades in college. Most importantly, don't let your good grades interfere with your learning.

44 Don't Freak Out over Finals

You've taken tests and written papers throughout your twelve or more years of prior schooling. You've obviously done fairly or very well on those exams in order for you to have been admitted to college. In all likelihood, you've also taken final exams for at least a few years. If you take a moment to think about it, you have as much experience in test taking as you do in almost any aspect of your life. Consider yourself an expert!

As the last weeks of the semester approach, there's always a buzz on campus about finals. "How many finals do you have?" "Are they spaced out over several days or bunched together?" "I hear that professor gives really hard finals." "I have only one final, but I've got three long papers due." "I've got to get at least a B on my final to get a decent grade." You should rise above this unfortunate level of anxiety that spreads through campus about finals.

You know how to do this. You make a finals schedule, a study guide for each class, and a study schedule to go with it. You figure out where you want to study—your room, the library, a lounge, an empty class-room. You arrange for study groups or you prepare by yourself. You review your notes, go over the texts, identify key themes, topics, information. You stay healthy by eating right and getting enough sleep. You reserve some free time to relax. You get to the exam a few minutes early, take a deep breath, complete the final, and give a sigh of relief.

If it's that easy, why does it seem so hard? The hardest part is psychological. While there is an elevated level of anxiety on campus about finals, it is still within normal limits. Where there is an unhealthy degree of anxiety, even a degree of frenzy, is in your college home, your residence hall. If you were in an apartment or house on campus, you'd be living with three or four others who had varying degrees of anxiety about their finals, just as they might about any exams. In the residence hall, however, and particularly in residence halls where most first-year students live, there's a fabricated and unhealthy level of anxiety because everyone around you—thirty, fifty, two hundred, or even a thousand students—is about to take his or her first set of college final exams.

All around you people are talking about their upcoming finals. It might be fun at first to have this shared experience, but it quickly becomes annoying and distracting, and it can also be unhealthy. The residence halls try their best to address the situation with round-the-clock quiet hours, study breaks, snacks, and various other distractions.

What you need to remember is that a final exam is just an exam. Be smart by anticipating that there will be a heightened degree of anxiety in the residence hall. Know that it's coming, but don't let it affect you. Focus on your studies, not the anxieties in the air. Eat well. Get rest. Avoid the all-nighter if at all possible. However, if you should feel overwhelmed at any point, go to the campus counseling office, where there are almost always extra staff on duty, walk-in appointments, and people ready to assist and support you at this point in the semester. Finals go by very quickly, and before you know it you'll be at home for a few days of work, rest, relaxation, and a much-needed change of pace.

45 Be Intellectually Honest: Don't Cheat

At college it's called "academic integrity." It is the academic equivalent of civil law. Academic integrity is essential to the entire enterprise of scholarly inquiry and intellectual exploration.

In college, cheating is like stealing. If you are caught cheating, you will be brought before an academic judiciary. You will face punishment that can range from a stern warning to a failing grade on a test or entire course, suspension, or expulsion.

The best and only advice about cheating is to never, ever do it.

Your purpose in college is to learn, and you will learn nothing from cheating. You are stealing someone else's ideas in order for you to get a better grade.

There are many views as to why a significant amount of cheating occurs on college campuses. Some people believe it just reflects the breakdown of basic values in society, a lack of respect for rules, peers, and authority. Others suggest that there is so much stress and competition to get top grades, particularly in the preprofessional programs, that students feel pressured to break the rules in order to fulfill their professional goals. Finally, some students unknowingly cheat, not being fully aware of what constitutes plagiarism.

Students cheat (and get caught) in any number of ways. They look over a classmate's shoulder during an exam to get an answer. They copy other students' papers. They buy papers over the Internet. They use pieces of other people's works without giving any citation. They set up computer programs to use other people's work to complete lab assignments and math problems. Faculty and university administrators know all the tricks of the trade and are quite adept at identifying student cheaters.

The question of academic integrity is a matter of personal integrity. The cheating habits you develop or maintain in college are likely to stay with you throughout your business life and personal relations. If you cheat because you feel unbearable stress in college, rest assured that the pressure will be that much more intense and stressful in the work world. Don't get started down this wrongheaded path. You are better than this. You don't want or need to get ahead by cheating.

Live your life honestly so you can wake up every morning proud of your life and proud of all your accomplishments. Examine your ethical makeup and your personal integrity. Set yourself on the right course in college, and it will serve you well throughout your entire life.

Expanding Your
Social Boundaries

46 Take Responsibility for the World around You

You bring a new set of eyes to the world around you. As a college student, you have the ability to see problems and opportunities that older people may not see so clearly. Each generation has the chance—even the responsibility—to learn from the past and present and to make changes to improve and sustain society for the future. This isn't a frivolous responsibility; it is one you should accept with respect, courage, and commitment.

College is a time when you get to think a lot about yourself—your development and growth, your personal ambitions, your relationships, and your academic success. It is actually quite important that you take the time necessary to think hard about the kind of person you want to be as an adult.

At the same time, it's just as important that you begin to see yourself as someone who can and should make a significant impact on the world around you. Just as there is a value in looking after your own well-being, as citizens of our communities, cities, nations, and world, we also need to look after the well-being of those around us.

There is, in fact, a long tradition in the United States and elsewhere of college students asking hard questions of college and political leaders about societal conditions. Those questions have often been linked to student activism and to taking a stand for moral principles.

There are a number of ways to think about this social responsibility. First, taking responsibility for others is a sign of moving from childhood, when you are the responsibility *of* others, to adulthood, when you are responsible *for* others. Second, taking responsibility for other people and for societal issues is a positive sign of empowerment, indicating that you consider yourself a full-fledged member of society and that you feel you have the motivation and power to actually contribute to the well-being of others and to create change in society. Third, it demonstrates that you have enough confidence in yourself to give of yourself to others.

How might you take responsibility for the world around you? There's a whole range of approaches, and you should find the ways that best fit your personality. One way to do this is through your personal relationships: how you relate to acquaintances, friends, even strangers. Do you interrupt racist or anti-Semitic jokes, do you behave respectfully toward the man or woman with whom you develop a romantic relationship, do you speak openly and honestly about people around you just as you would if they weren't present?

Others may find that they can give back to society most constructively through community service and volunteer work, by tutoring in a school, by volunteering in a hospital, or by serving in an organization and on its committees. Still others decide to run for political office, to vote in elections, to write letters to the editor, or to contest college administrators' or political leaders' decisions.

Decide what approach best fits who you are. This process may take some time, but look at the world around you and work to make it a better place than when you entered it.

47 Withhold Assumptions about People

You walk onto campus and you see someone looking at you. You've never met this person, but you can tell that he's sizing you up. He's drawing a mental picture of who you are, putting you into a small and limiting box.

No one would question that he is drawing a distorted, stereotypical picture of you. At the same time, the truth is that almost all of us do the same kind of sizing up of other people around us, making judgments and drawing on stereotypical images of all kinds of unique individuals around us.

So what's the problem? The problem is that when others do this to us or we do the same to others around us, we lose sight of the very special, unique characteristics that each of us prides ourselves on as individuals. We erase the individuality and soul of each person around us. And, as is usually the case, we miss out on opportunities to meet all kinds of amazing people.

Especially for the vast majority of college students, who come from homogeneous backgrounds, the stereotyping and dismissal of people based on physical characteristics represents a tremendous opportunity lost. A woman with blond hair—haven't we been taught throughout our lives a negative, stereotypical image about that person's intelligence? A man with an earring—is that truly supposed to give us clear insight into that person's personality and values? A southern accent in a northern state or vice versa—do any of us really believe that we can learn anything substantive about someone's personality from an accent?

And yet so many college students are inclined to go ahead and forge friendships with or avoid people based on these grand assumptions based on so little (mis)information. Some of us will set high or low expectations of people based on what region of the country they come from. "Oh, you're from New York? Or Chicago? Well, I've got you all figured out. I know what you're all about." Surely, if we paused for just an instant, all of us would know that this one person cannot possibly be exactly like the other millions of people in New York City.

The sad part is that far too many of your fellow college students may be judging you in the same way. How wrong and simplistic can they be! Yet all these college students are supposed to be so smart!

My hope is that you will be just a little bit smarter than they are. Try this. Every time you meet a new person at college, withhold your assumptions about them. Try to actually meet and get to know the person behind the handbag, the T-shirt, the skin color, the city they come from, the accent, or the weight and height. Get to know each person's individual values, history, aspirations, humor, and friends. Find out about others just as you'd hope they would want to learn about you.

I think this approach not only will give you a chance to make real, lasting friendships with people from all backgrounds but along the way will help you to learn to like yourself a lot more as you give yourself and others a chance to grow beyond the little boxes into which we paint ourselves.

48 Participate in Intergroup Dialogue

Imagine this experience in college: white students in a small class talking with students of color; gay students in conversation with straight students; men and women talking honestly together; students meeting with their peers from different religious backgrounds; U.S. students engaged in activities with international students. You could be participating in these intergroup dialogues.

Across the country, more and more universities are establishing programs to help students engage in in-depth, serious conversations with fellow students from different social backgrounds.

It's hard for many students like you to find a safe space to ask one another the really hard questions about race, gender, sexual orientation, religious difference, and so on. If you're like the great majority of entering college students, it's highly unlikely that you've had the experience of a deep and sustained conversation with others about the important and enduring issues of difference, commonalities, equalities, and inequalities based on our social identities.

Most students, like you, are very eager for these conversations, yet we all know how hard it is to speak openly about our society's longstanding divisions and conflicts. Intergroup dialogues on college campuses—organized through courses, workshops, or retreats—are structured to give you and other students a chance to meet one another as individuals and as members of various social identity groups, develop a degree of trust in the dialogue group, and build a safe space in which to engage the truly difficult issues that so often divide us.

Students talk about intergroup dialogues as being transformative experiences. What is so exciting about them is that because they give you a chance to open the doors to the potential of a diverse society and the dream of American democracy. It's a chance to participate in grassroots democracy, an updated version of the nineteenth-century New England town hall meeting, where citizens took active control and responsibility for the life of the community and the democratic society. Instead of being held back by the fear and invisible walls that keep people apart, students who participate in dialogues are able to personally engage with their peers on campus and embrace a world that brings all people together.

Another advantage of intergroup dialogue is that, as research findings demonstrate, if you as a student engage with people from different backgrounds, you will learn and understand in deeper and more complex ways than your peers who remain safely in their own comfort zones. Finally, you are more likely to find that the professional world that awaits you as a graduating senior will be looking for someone just like you, a person who can work effectively with people from all different backgrounds as employees, coworkers, and supervisors.

Don't miss this opportunity—it's a chance for you to gain the full benefit of an undergraduate education and to become an active participant and leader in our democratic society.

BILL WALTERS—*"Stepping Outside My World."*
Bill Walters chose his college for two reasons: (1) it has a great academic reputation and, (2) it is a distance from his home and has a much more diverse student body than his small town. Bill grew up in a bedroom community in a small city, surrounded by white, middle-class students like himself. His parents were happily married and worked, his dad as a salesman and his mom as an administrative assistant.

Bill was very popular and loved his hometown, but he also read a lot and knew that there was a bigger world outside the comfort of his home. He was among the first in his town to attend this particular college, and it hadn't been an easy decision for him. It took some courage to leave behind the safety of familiar friends and neighbors to explore the world through college.

When Bill arrived at college, he was so pleased to meet people from different states, different religions, and different racial and ethnic backgrounds. That's what he had been looking for. But, despite everyone's initial friendliness, there seemed to be an element of superficiality to all the friendliness. Oh, everyone was nice enough, really, but Bill didn't feel particularly welcome at some of the events that were held for other students, like the Black orientation, the Pan-Asian barbeque, or the Jewish student movie night.

Bill went to church on Sunday and felt at home in the service, though he did miss his church at home. He also decided to participate in fraternity rush in order to make some close friends. All of this provided some comfort to Bill, but he was aware that his friends were all like the ones he knew at home. All were white, all were middle-class, all were Christian.

One day, a close friend from home, Mark, made a comment that took Bill by surprise: "Why did you go so far away to college if you were just going to hang around with all the same kind of people like back here at home? Maybe you should come back home where your best friends are and think about transferring to the city college."

That comment shocked Bill. Wow! Bill felt really close to Mark and other friends from home, but he had no intention of leaving his college. That wasn't at all what he wanted. It wasn't as if Bill didn't want to have all the good friends he had made, but Mark's comment was a reminder that Bill really did want to meet new friends, including students from many different backgrounds. That was, in fact, one of the important reasons why he had chosen this school. College, he had always believed, was about meeting the world—not just in books but in the diversity of the campus. Still, Bill wondered how he was going to meet any of these new people.

Over the next few weeks, Bill made a point of reaching out and extending himself. Although it felt awkward and uncomfortable to him, he sat down at a lunch table in the residence hall cafeteria with a few of the African American students that he had met at orientation. Without hesitation, they included him in their conversation about classes. When the Jewish students on his floor were talking about a party they planned to go to that weekend, he asked if he could join them, and they were happy to have him along. Even though his church group was getting together to watch the college's football game, Bill decided to stay in the residence hall to watch it at the party the hall council had organized, and he was thrilled to see all the different groups of people gather together to support the team.

As Bill took these steps to branch out, he also found himself trying other new activities. He went to the mass meeting for students wanting to try out for the school newspaper. He attended an evening lecture on the role of business in foreign affairs. He talked to one of his professors to see if he could help him out with his research project on health care in Latin America.

What really thrilled Bill as he reached out and experimented with these new friends and opportunities was that he found that he hadn't had to give up his own traditions or practices to be with others. In fact, his friends from other religions asked if they could come join him when he went to church on Sunday. His new friends from the Philippines and Chile wanted to know all about his own French and Greek ethnic heritage. Bill had long talks with a friend whose parents were divorced, with guys who came from wealthy families and with students who worked twenty-five hours a week and even then barely kept up with school loans.

Bill found what he was looking for in college. He hadn't lost the comfort and safety of his home and neighborhood, his own bubble; rather, he had found that he could also have safety in a much wider comfort zone. He didn't have to choose *one or the other but settled into a fulfilling and meaningful life in a much bigger world than his hometown had allowed. Bill had made the right choice for himself.*

49   Examine Your Social Identity

You will find yourself at college with a whole new set of people surrounding you—new friends, new classmates, new teachers, new adults. You have an opportunity to explore, experiment, establish, and assert who you are, what your identity is, and who you want to be in life.

The values you hold, what you intrinsically believe, and how you see and define yourself, regardless of anyone else's viewpoint, should be the most important factors in establishing your identity. The views of outsiders become particularly important when they come from people you know and trust. But even those views should stand apart from your own independent and internal sense of your values and identity.

However, in addition to your special and unique individual identity, you also have various social identities. This means that your individual identity is linked to the social identity of many other people. These social identities range from ethnic identity to racial identity, religious identity, economic class identity, gender identity, sexual orientation identity, and so forth. For many of you, your social identity includes more than one group within each of these categories, such as more than one ethnic, racial, or religious identity.

Social identities are very significant in our lives. You may choose not to embrace the values, histories, cultures, traditions, and other beliefs and practices associated with a group that is part of your social identity. However, people and institutions outside the group will typically hold attitudes and act in certain ways toward you simply on the basis of your social identity, regardless of your degree of commitment to the group. The history of our civilization and of this country tells repeated stories of oppression and injustices toward people based solely on their social identities.

Social identities matter. Even though everyone at your college has in common the fact that they are outstanding students attending the same college and taking similar classes, there will be strong pressures to try to limit the kinds of people with whom you become friends and associate based solely on their social identities. We all have made assumptions and often acted in particular ways toward other individuals based strictly on their race, gender, religion, and economic class.

At the same time, if you are clear and thoughtful about your privileges and social disadvantages that are based on your various social identities, you may have the courage and conviction to cross and challenge some of these barriers. In so doing, you will find that you are able to both explore a much broader set of friendships than you had while growing up and help to establish a world based on social justice for people from all backgrounds.

50 Do Community Service

Getting involved in community work during college is important for many reasons. First, you will learn a great deal about yourself as a result of meeting and interacting with people different from you. Those contacts will cause you to reflect on yourself, your family, your racial and class background, and the privileges and challenges that you have faced in your life. Second, you will learn an enormous amount about the community with which you work in terms of the people, their racial and economic backgrounds, and the meaning and challenges they find in their lives. Third, you will begin to become a deeper thinker by beginning to see things from the perspectives of people who view the world through a different lens from yours.

These experiences are important, too, because you will be helping the community by making an important contribution. Most students don't realize just how important their impact is, whether it involves tutoring or mentoring children, visiting the elderly, or helping in an office. Community agencies depend on their volunteers' contributions, and while college students often think that what they do is inconsequential, children, seniors, and agency administrators all note the absence any time a volunteer doesn't show up when expected. It's an important lesson to realize that people depend on you and that you have a lot to offer.

In college you should recognize the distinction between community service and community service-learning. In high school, many students do community service out of a strong personal or ethical commitment, because it makes them feel good, in order to fulfill school requirements, or to build a good résumé for college applications. What distinguishes service from service-learning is that service-learning requires you to read and reflect about your experience—it becomes part of your intellectual work at college in addition to service work.

What you may learn during this opportunity for reflection, first, are the many types of service and the reasons for doing it. Service and participation in one's community are an important part of being a citizen in a democratic society. To remain strong, democracies need their citizens to be active and involved. People do community service for a variety of reasons, ranging from how good it sometimes feels to help others, to a sense of obligation for those with more privileges to help others who are less fortunate, to religious notions of charity.

Others do community service because they feel they are partners with people from all segments of society in creating a more just society for all. They may want to go beyond being charitable to making the changes in the social structures of society that will help reduce the need for food kitchens and after-school tutors, and which will help create more jobs and better schools. These are the kinds of things you will want to reflect on in a service-learning project.

Another important lesson in service-learning is the deeper understanding you will gain about social issues and identities, including social justice and the content of the service project. As a student, you will have a chance to think more about your place in society, your privileges and the challenges you face based on whether you are a member of a majority or minority social group. You will undoubtedly learn more about yourself as you learn more about the people you are serving in the community.

51   Participate in Alternative Spring Break

One of the most novel innovations in higher education in recent years is what is called Alternative Spring Break. Instead of spending spring break flying to a beach town for revelry, thousands of students now use this time to work for a community in great need. It provides very useful service to the community and is an opportunity for deep learning for you.

The concept of Alternative Spring Break is important. The message is not just that one should look for an alternative to spring break. It also speaks to the voice of students saying that there is an alternative to always focusing on one's pleasure and self. Alternative Spring Break says it is important to care and give of oneself to others in need.

Like all volunteering and community service experiences, the learning takes place most effectively if you take time to prepare for the community with which you will work and if you take time to reflect on the experience. Be sure that you have these opportunities prior to and after the actual work at the site.

An important part of the attraction of this alternative is the close bond that develops among the participants. Students go in groups of ten to fifteen to Alternative Spring Break sites. They live, work, and socialize together. When a group really clicks, the relationships that grow and the learning that takes place are very powerful.

There are costs involved because students usually travel to cities and sites outside the region of their college. Thus, there are travel costs, food costs, and lodging costs, although lodging is usually arranged through the community site at local homes, community centers, or religious centers. As a group, students learn and do fund-raising for several months in advance in order to cover their expenses.

A wide range of sites can be selected. Students might work with the homeless, people with HIV/AIDS, children in failing schools, women's shelters, food kitchens, and so on. Students often work with ethnic and racial communities that are different from their own background. The college should be expected to do a thorough job of researching all these sites before arranging to send students.

No one will get famous for participating in Alternative Spring Break. You shouldn't expect any of the media attention, on campus and on national TV, that the traditional wild spring break parties get. Nevertheless, many students tell me that Alternative Spring Break is a transformative experience, the highlight of their school year.

52 Collaborate with Your Peers

To succeed in your personal and professional life, you will need to have good skills in collaboration so that you can work effectively with people you like and befriend, those you don't know well or don't like, those who come from similar or different backgrounds from yours, and even those who hold different or competing values and personal styles than you.

High schools and colleges increasingly require students to work on joint projects, participate in study groups, and write papers together. The research on study groups clearly demonstrates that students, both those more and less advanced, learn more in groups than by exclusively studying alone.

If you're like many other students, I have no doubt that you're thinking that study groups and group projects don't always feel like they're very worthwhile. They can take more time, more social involvement, and more effort and can result in occasional struggles with one individual who does not come ready to do an equal share of the work. All of this reflects real life in the workplace and community, and these are important though sometimes unpleasant and painful skills to learn.

The key is that you want these collaborative projects to work well and efficiently, not badly. How do you do that? First, you have to come prepared. Second, you have to come with a readiness to learn and cooperate. Third, you must be prepared to be open to working and learning in a manner of equality with people who may have different learning and working styles, who may have different goals and ambitions, and who come from backgrounds different from yours.

One of the common problems in work projects is that people often reinforce societal stereotypes in their collaborations. In math study groups, for example, men sometimes have lower expectations for the ability of women in the group and seek to dominate the discussion. Be sure to check your stereotypes and assumptions at the door—come with openness and high expectations for all participants.

It is important right from the start to determine how to share work responsibilities early in the project. If you're doing a group research project and paper, decide early on who will do which parts of the research—library research, data collection, interviews, and so on—and who will take responsibility for the writing. You may decide that each person will write a section of the paper, but then someone will need to rewrite so the paper has one voice. Another option is for a person who does less of the data collection to take responsibility for writing a draft of the paper and then have others revise and rewrite. It's always important to set strict timelines and check-in dates to be sure that all the required work is getting completed with high standards.

Study groups work the same way. Schedule meetings early and frequently. Decide who will facilitate each study group and who is responsible for presenting which aspects of the study preparation. Sometimes everyone will need to be responsible for everything; other times you will want to share responsibilities. Decide early on the ground rules for continued participation and under what conditions a person may be asked to leave the group.

Collaboration skills come into play in almost everything you do.

Developing these skills will serve you well in your personal and professional relationships, your learning, your growth and love of life, and your professional and career development.

53 Learn a Second (or Third) Language

Many U.S. citizens wonder why there is even a need for second–language instruction. After all, English is spoken throughout the United States and in many parts of the world. My advice to you is to stop wondering and start studying a second language. It's in your own best interest.

The world grows smaller and more interconnected each day. For you, as today's college student and tomorrow's professional, the nations of the globe will seem much more like the proverbial global village than anyone can begin to imagine now. Further, the multilingual global village increasingly resides not just in foreign countries but within the U.S. borders as well.

The speed of travel, the instant communication of the global Internet, the rapid expansion of global business networks, and the natural resources that know no boundaries and that we increasingly share across the globe will lead us to have much more frequent and consistent contact with people everywhere. Literature, movies, politics, business, and trade cross our borders every day whether or not we choose to acknowledge the massive interdependence of the peoples throughout the world.

It has always been the case, and it is no different today, that we know we can understand and communicate better across cultures if we know the language of different cultures. Language in translation is considerably different and less rich than the original. The precise meanings, the cultural understandings, and the delicate nuances of language cannot be adequately captured in translation.

Much of the world already speaks more than one language. As you increasingly think of yourself as a global citizen as well as a citizen of a particular nation, you will need to speak a second language to keep up. Even the United States itself is increasingly becoming a bilingual or even multilingual nation, and to move comfortably across the business and cultural sectors within this society, you should be conversant in more than one language.

When you travel abroad, you will want to speak that country's language. When you apply for a job or a promotion, you will not want to be held back because you can't speak the language of your business partners and clients. When you watch a movie, you will not want to be relegated to reading subtitles. When you read newspapers online from many different nations, you will want to read the original text. When you meet friends and colleagues from different backgrounds, you will want to freely converse and communicate deeply with them in both your and their first languages.

When you receive your college degree, you will want to think of yourself as an educated individual. Be sure to learn a second language so you will have no doubts about that claim.

54 Study Abroad

Study abroad has long been acknowledged as an important part of an undergraduate experience. In our global society today, studying abroad is more important than ever. Don't miss out on this learning opportunity.

Surprisingly, the number of students who go abroad during college remains relatively small, and the number who take full educational advantage of this remarkable opportunity is much smaller still.

Study abroad is important because it gives you the opportunity to both see how others live, and also to see your way of life, values, studies, and national and cultural society from an entirely different perspective. You are likely to encounter new cultures, values, and foods as well as different languages, news reports, economic systems, and governmental structures. You will find that people in other countries don't always view your world or way of life as the centerpiece of how they see the world and value life.

These encounters with the new and the different and your immersion in such a society allow you to grow and learn and see much more broadly than you could ever imagine. Living and studying in another country, like other encounters with diversity, allow you to examine your life, values, and perspectives and to reaffirm, challenge, deepen, and problematize them with all the new experiences and lessons you will gather from another country.

Importantly, studying abroad can also prepare you well for a professional career that requires you to be culturally aware and sensitive to the perspectives and experiences of people living in different parts of the globe.

The most traditional approach is to go on a college-sponsored study abroad program for a semester or a year. If you go on a program that your college sponsors, it is sometimes easier to arrange credit transfer and financial aid, but a great many students go abroad on other colleges' programs and easily transfer credits and even save money. Meet with your academic advisor well in advance of your trip to make certain that your study plan will fit well with the requirements of your academic studies, and make sure to keep abreast of any safety or travel advisories.

Other ways to study abroad include summer study at various universities, theme-based programs such as theater/Shakespeare programs in England, biological/natural resources programs in Latin America, or language immersion programs in Israel or Egypt. Some students choose to pursue a semester at sea.

In recent years, even more innovative programs have emerged. Increasingly, colleges offer small groups of students an opportunity to travel abroad with a faculty member to work together on a research project or educational initiative. Other colleges now help students identify opportunities to work on a community service-learning project in another country. Still other students participate in internship experiences in business, nonprofit organizations, and government agencies in various countries around the world.

It is important to think about your purpose in studying abroad. Your experience will be most beneficial and transformative if you allow yourself to meet the native residents, speak the language, and fully immerse yourself in the culture. Since many students travel on a U.S.-sponsored college study abroad program, it takes initiative on your part to avoid having an exclusively American experience even though you are in a foreign country. These students may have a great time abroad, because after all, it is fun to be on vacation, but they miss out on the deeper learning opportunity that is possible through study abroad.

Safety is certainly a consideration in travel abroad. Be sure to keep in touch with your campus study abroad office so that you are notified of any travel advisories for countries in which you wish to study.

Go study abroad, enjoy, and be safe while you experience as much as you can. Just be sure to make it a rich learning experience.

―――

BESS SIMS—*"Crossing the Economic Divide."*

Bess Sims let out a gasp to her best friend, Meghan. She squeezed Meghan's hand and hurriedly walked past the crowd gathered on the campus commons to go to her class. "Did you see what those girls were wearing? That purse alone must have cost hundreds of dollars!"

Bess came to college from a small, rural town. Her father had wanted her to stay close by and attend the local college with kids from neighboring towns who shared the same family values, religion, and way of life. But Bess's mom thought Bess ought to spread her wings and explore the world a bit. She knew Bess was a very bright girl and was certain that at some point or another Bess would leave their small town for a broader cultural experience. Why not try exploring the world in a very good college, with the structure of challenging classes, with a couple of friends from high school, and within a few hours driving distance of home?

The first thing Bess noticed when she arrived on campus was how much stuff people had brought with them. Bess's family wasn't poor, by any means, but the students in her residence hall had brought microwaves, TVs, computers, top model stereo systems, and clothes—so much fancy clothing she could hardly believe it. Bess's family had taken a big shopping trip to the large discount mall about forty miles from her home, and her dad had frowned all day about all the new outfits that she and her mom had picked out. Still, she wasn't prepared for this.

And, she marveled, too, at the brand-new cars that it seemed so many students were driving. Bess had worked after school during her last three years of high school to help pay for a ten-year-old used car—and she had felt pretty great about that accomplishment. But these kids were driving cars that looked like they had come right off the new car lot, and they were a lot fancier than what her parents were driving!

For the most part, Bess didn't mind seeing that some of the students had so much fancy stuff. After all, she dreamed about having those things, too, and was hoping that by going to college she would be able to have more things like that as she got older. And many of the kids on her hall who had more things were really nice and weren't really materialistic at all. Still, it seemed like some kids wouldn't even talk to her if she wasn't carrying the right purse or wearing the right shoes. Sometimes that made her angry or even feel bad about herself, but most of the time she just ignored their vanity and felt sorry for their shallow values.

Late one night, Bess was hanging out on the hall with some of the girls, eating pizza that they had all ordered in. Bess and Johanna got into a conversation about everything from religion to politics to fashion. It seemed like they covered every topic imaginable, and they didn't get to bed till nearly four in the morning.

Johanna lived in the downtown area of the big city in the state, was super friendly and, it seemed to Bess, had lived her life entirely differently in most every respect. She had gone to elite, private schools her entire life, had traveled abroad several times, and her parents were high-powered professionals, a doctor and a corporate lawyer. Yet the two of them shared so much in common it was amazing. Johanna didn't even seem to notice that Bess was from a small town and had only once or twice visited the downtown area where Johanna lived.

Johanna wore clothes that looked like Bess's, but there was a striking difference. All of Johanna's things were top-of-the-line name brands, and each blouse, pair of jeans, and purse cost many times more than Bess's discount mall clothing. Yet although Johanna liked to shop, as did Bess, Johanna didn't really care much about designer clothing; she told Bess that she just shopped in the stores in her neighborhood—which were definitely upscale—and therefore everything she owned was expensive and designer. She wasn't showy, just wealthy. Bess *knew that if she saw someone like Johanna in one of her classes, she would have sized her up and written her off in a minute. But now that they were friends, Bess questioned her own attitude.*

It turned out that Johanna not only had more expensive clothes, but she also had different ideas about almost everything they loved to talk about—religion, music, sports, family, and relationships. Strangely, that didn't seem to matter to either of them. What they really appreciated about one another was that they could talk so easily and openly to one another. Bess and Johanna listened and appreciated each other for who they were, not what they wore or where they came from. And, as they came to be best friends over time, they each adapted, learned from one another, visited each other's homes, and learned not to judge so harshly.

55 Take Democracy Seriously: Participate Actively in Civic Life

Those of us who have grown up in a democratic society often assume that our way of government will go on forever and ever. But a growing chorus of scholars warns that democracies are actually fairly fragile enterprises that may not endure unless they are cared for and looked after.

That's our job, and that's your job.

Here are a list of things you can do to make your democracy stronger and enhance your college experience and the reasons why these activities are so important. Remember, our democracy is of the people, by the people, and for the people—and you are the people!

Vote! When only a few people vote, it means that a small elite is getting to make the decisions for you about who runs our cities, our states, and our country. That's not very democratic.

Get involved and participate! Run for office in your student government. Attend a city council meeting and voice your opinion. Go to your town's school board meetings. Write a letter to the editor of your newspaper. Fewer and fewer citizens are involved in local politics. Again, that means that a small minority are making decisions about how we should live our lives!

Join organizations! You don't need to be political, but you need to be involved in the community. Join a student club, an environmental organization, an outing group, a choir, a sports team, a religious or ethnic group, or a social organization. Citizen involvement in community organizations and clubs has dropped sharply; instead, people are sitting home alone watching TV or spending more time at work. An engaged citizenry makes for a strong democracy by sharing news, discussing ideas, and building community.

Do community service! Make the concerns of your neighborhood and surrounding towns and cities your business. Yes, it does take all of us to keep the nation's democracy healthy and vibrant for this generation and those to follow. If we don't care about the people in our community, state, nation, we can't expect that elected officials will care about you or your neighbors. Citizens in a democratic nation look after other citizens and take responsibility for the good of the whole.

Get a good education! Democracies need educated citizens—citizens and leaders who can think critically, reason analytically, and size up complex problems from many different perspectives. An uneducated, uninformed citizenry is more likely to follow demagogues and fail to challenge bad ideas from wrongheaded leaders. College students like you, who will be well educated and involved in society, are our nation's best hope for a strong, diverse democracy.

56 Think about Social Justice

Have you ever thought about what you would do if you had the power to make the world a better place? You should give this some consideration during your college years because you'll find that you have much more power to influence change than you might imagine.

When people talk about social justice, issues such as hunger, homelessness, health care, and discrimination often come to mind. What areas do you think need change to create a more just world for everyone?

While it may not be difficult to identify the many areas that need change, the reasons for injustices and the solutions for creating more just conditions are often very complex. Sometimes the problem is as simple as bad people doing bad or even horrific things to others. Usually, however, the problem lies in the historic and structural conditions that maintain inequalities and injustices within societies or across national borders.

As a person embarking on a college education, you will have an opportunity to investigate and better understand the underlying causes of injustice in the world. It may be frustrating, to some extent, to learn how difficult it is to find comprehensive solutions. However, your new knowledge and insights may empower you to take action to work for the changes necessary to bring about a more just society.

One of the lessons you will learn in your studies is how powerful a person you are, in relative terms, just because you've received a college education. Globally, your college education places you among an elite group in the world. This is a privilege and opportunity you should not take lightly.

You might wonder how you could be a member of an elite group when you look about and see so many with so much more than you have. Surprisingly, sometimes it's precisely when we do have power and influence that we don't realize what we have.

Your college education gives you rights and responsibilities that comparatively few people worldwide possess. While you may be thinking that you're not so exceptionally smart or privileged given your place in your high school class rank or the fact that you may not have gained admission to your first-choice college, the fact of the matter is that you are among the most highly educated people in the world.

Think about what good you want to do with your education. What does social justice mean to you? What can you do to make a change in the world, whether it be among your friends and family, in your community, your city, your state, or your nation or across national borders? How can you take advantage of the power and privilege that your college education confers to make the world a more just place for everyone?

57 Be a Boundary-Crosser

The next generation of leaders will be boundary-crossers. You should learn to be one as part of your college education.

Boundary-crossers can move easily across groups and categories of people. They have the attitude, skills, and mind-set that allow them to transcend the social barriers that most people don't dare cross.

Boundary-crossers are respectful of other people and are interested in their commonalities and differences. They are good listeners but are just as willing and ready to fully engage. They are open and honest.

Boundary-crossers see connections and opportunities for collaboration. They are expert at linking people together locally, nationally, and globally. They don't see walls, they see pathways.

Boundary-crossers are comfortable with people, ideas, and organizations. They have a natural curiosity about all kinds of subject matter, and they find people's lives and stories intriguing. They are problem-solvers, connectors, and bridge-builders. They don't need to be at the top of the hierarchy, but we'd all be a lot better off if more of them were. They can move easily across the different ranks of personnel within an organization.

As a college student, you can both learn the skills of boundary-crossers and practice those skills. By intentionally working to expand your comfort zone, you will begin to gain a level of ease being with people from different social backgrounds. By getting to know the persons behind particular viewpoints, you will appreciate how even well-educated, well-meaning, and very likeable people can differ dramatically on politics and issues of intellectual interest. By taking a broad array of courses across various disciplines, you will gain an understanding about why and how different people can be so intrigued by and even passionate about topics that you hadn't even heard of.

In college you will find the same walls set up to divide people and organizations that exist in society at large. Students will divide themselves up by social identity groups. Those students with different political views from their neighbors won't associate with each other except to shout their views louder than the next person. Student leaders of one organization won't even think of the opportunities that exist by collaborating with the organization next door, let alone acting in anything but a competitive manner.

You can be different. You can bring people and organizations together. You can be friends with individuals from different political parties as easily as you can be friends with people who have different majors. You can engage your peers regarding contentious issues but still leave the discussion with respect for one another. You can find common ground and opportunity in difference.

In becoming a boundary-crosser, you will find that your learning increases exponentially by moving across and between boundaries. You will find that your friendships are as wide as they are deep. You will learn to see value and opportunity in almost every person, idea, issue, and organization you encounter. You will be prepared to take on leadership roles in your family and community. In civic life, in business, and throughout your professional life, you will be a much-sought-after person. You will see the world more positively, and you will make the world a more positive place in which to live.

Campus Life

58   Learn Outside the Classroom

Some of the most important lessons you will learn in college will take place outside the classroom.

You can learn from every individual you encounter and every activity you participate in, no matter where or when those interactions take place, as long as you make a point of reflecting on those encounters and experiences. College is an environment of intentional learning, and you should begin to think of yourself as an intentional learner. Maximize your opportunities for learning as deeply and as broadly as possible from all your college-related experiences.

You should consider a variety of categories of learning outside the classroom. Consider first what may seem to be the easiest and most natural, hanging out with friends. At college, you have a chance to broaden your scope of friends. If you step outside your room, you are likely to meet individuals who come from a much wider variety of racial, ethnic, religious, class, and sexual orientation backgrounds than you have previously been exposed to or been friendly with. Get to know these people. Make friends with them. In time, open up yourself to them about your background and learn about theirs.

Second, get involved. Play on sports teams. Join the newspaper, the drama club, the chemistry club, your ethnic group organization, or your residence hall council. Volunteer for a community service project, take on an internship, find a job. All of these activities will give you insight into how organizations and people within organizations work in different sectors of society. Are the organizations highly structured or unstructured, hierarchical or authority sharing? Do people involved work competitively or collaboratively, do they do things together outside of work, or does everyone go their own way immediately after a meeting or the job is done?

Third, attend all sorts of campus events, including those that are social, educational, and cultural. Go to a football or hockey game. Attend the opera, a chamber orchestra concert, a comedian's performance, or a musical production. Go to a debate about global warming, a speaker on race relations, a talk about the human genome, a workshop on getting along with your roommate, a documentary about endangered species. Go by yourself, with a friend, with a large group from your residence hall. You will be exposed to a wide range of life from many different vantage points. Enjoy yourself, and learn about the world around you.

Finally, get involved in campus and community organizations to learn leadership skills. Run for an office in student government. Take a position in a departmental club. Train to become a student facilitator for an intergroup dialogue class. Be a site leader one day a week for the local food kitchen. Let a faculty member or dean know that you'd like to be a student representative on a faculty committee. Attend leadership workshops or retreats. You will learn about different kinds of leadership, where your strengths lie, and how you like to participate in organizations.

College is an all-day, every-day learning experience, and you should take advantage of the immense learning opportunities available both inside and outside of the classroom.

59   Get Along with Your Roommate

You'll be happiest if you start with positive yet modest expectations for your relationship with your roommate. You may hope for a perfect match, but you'll be more realistic if you anticipate that you'll have a reasonably respectful and civil relationship. Remember, you will spend eight to ten months in a small space, almost entirely filled with beds, desks, and dressers, together with a person (or persons) you've never met previously. The odds are on your side to have a perfectly good relationship, but don't count on perfect.

Students have lots of fantasies about their college roommates. You may have heard stories or watched TV shows where roommates are best friends and confidants. It does happen, it would be wonderful if it did, and it very well could. You may be thinking that you'll have similar tastes in room decoration, share values about neatness and cleanliness, and have good taste in friends. Your hope is that you'll share fears, celebrate successes, stay up late at night talking, and eat popcorn together watching favorite movies.

As hopeful but unlikely as this scenario is, it is just as unlikely that you and your roommate will be the very worst of matches. Your worst fears, that your roommate is a drug dealer, doesn't go to class, takes your things without asking, and is generally rude and disrespectful, are so unlikely that it's not worth giving much thought.

The actual experience of most students is a modestly positive one. You and your roommate are likely to get along just fine, although there may be some bumps in the road. You probably won't be each other's closest friends in the world, but you will share the experiences of one of your most memorable years. You will be able to negotiate most issues, such as differences about noise levels when one is sleeping, study time, and how to divide up the refrigerator. You may even end up liking and befriending some of your roommate's good friends.

It is critical that you approach your relationship with your roommate with respect, sensitivity, and civility. You have to learn to listen to his or her point of view, speak up for yourself and your views, speak openly and honestly, negotiate differences directly, and talk through any problems or disagreements.

Call your roommate during the summer before college to begin getting to know one another. Don't rush to decorate your room the day you move in without waiting to talk with your new roommate. Expect that he or she will have some different lifestyle habits and some different values from you. He may stay up late to study, while you go to bed early to wake up for eight o'clock classes. She may have five siblings and shared a room at home, while you have no siblings and have always had your own room. Your roommate will likely be different in some social identity, be it race, religion, class, ethnicity, or sexual orientation. Don't even think about the idea of rejecting a roommate because he or she comes from a different background (usually race). Be open to those differences, learn from them, and celebrate them.

It's not a good idea to room with your best friend from high school.

Yes, it can work in some cases, but more often best friends stay best friends when they don't live together.

Be the wonderful, kind, agreeable person you are, and your roommate is likely to respond in kind.

60 Enjoy Life in the Residence Hall

For students living on campus, much of your first year of college will take place in your new home, the college residence hall. You should plan to make the most of the experience.

You will want, of course, to make friends in your residence hall. Hopefully, you and other students on your floor and elsewhere in the hall will go to meals together, go to social events, and walk to class together in the morning. Enjoy this rare opportunity to have so many friends living together under one roof.

You need to be on good behavior in the residence hall. You need to be respectful of others and work toward building a healthy and strong community on your floor and in your building. You will be sharing a bathroom with many others, so clean up after yourself (and be sure to thank the housekeeping person who does the thorough cleanup on your floor every day). In your room, put your trash and recycling in the proper bins. When you play music, keep the sound within the confines of your own room. Be sensitive to the different musical tastes of people on your floor.

Your resident advisor (RA) is a person you will want to meet on move-in day. The RA is an upper-class student who lives on your floor and whose job it is to be there for you whenever you need help. See the

RA if you need to find out tips about campus life, if you have problems with a roommate or someone on the floor and have difficulty resolving the issue among yourselves, or if you have questions about how to access college resources.

Living in a residence hall is one of the best opportunities you will ever have to expand your social boundaries. Hopefully, you will have a chance to meet people from many different social identity groups and all parts of the country and world. Be sure to take advantage of this opportunity. Once you live outside of the residence halls, you won't have this opportunity again.

Students almost universally complain about food in the residence hall. It's a tradition. The truth, though, is that residence hall food these days is plentiful, varied, and quite tasty. At most colleges, you will have your choice of entrees, salad bar, breakfast foods, soft drinks, and desserts at every meal, and all prepared for you. No cooking, no dishwashing. Your biggest challenge will not be that you can't find food to eat but that you will have to limit yourself. It would get monotonous to eat every meal every day even at your favorite restaurant. So, go ahead and complain about dorm food if you must, but tell the dining hall staff the truth—the food's pretty great, and you really appreciate the fact that they're cooking and you're not. And make your parent(s) happy by saying that you miss home cooking. They'll feel good knowing that you have not forgotten them.

Finally, college residence halls work very hard to be educational centers not just dormitories, hostels, or apartments. Take advantage of the residential colleges, living-learning programs, educational activities, faculty speakers, and volunteer activities that are organized through the residence hall. Remember to learn from every experience in college, both curricular and cocurricular.

EDGAR HERNANDEZ — *"Vote for Me! Your Next President of the United States!"*

Don't underestimate Edgar Hernandez. Edgar isn't a cocky guy, but he is a man on a mission. He has his mind set. Edgar Hernandez is on the road to becoming the first Hispanic president of the United States!

Edgar grew up in a wealthy and largely white suburb of Chicago. He is a natural charmer. Handsome, smart, popular, athletic, and very ambitious—that is Edgar Hernandez in a nutshell. He was president of his high school, star receiver on his team's state championship football team, and winner of all kinds of awards and prizes. Edgar excelled in history and English, completed several AP courses, and received lots of offers for college admissions. Edgar has lots of friends, both male and female.

When Edgar arrived at college, he immediately looked for leadership opportunities. Edgar wasn't really shocked, but he couldn't help but notice that lots of other students on campus had been leaders at their high schools and also had high expectations for becoming campus leaders. The college had lots of bright, assertive, popular students—just like him.

But Edgar was not deterred. Actually, he thrived on the success of others and thought it was great to be among such a talented group of students. Edgar got situated in his classes, looked around campus a bit to see what opportunities existed, and then jumped in.

Academically, Edgar enrolled in an undergraduate research program in political polling, in which he got to work on a project with a leading national pollster. His primary goal, of course, was to get to know a faculty member on a personal basis. He also took a first-year seminar in history, a small class of fifteen students, where he came to know his professor and fellow students individually.

Politically, the opportunities were enormous. Edgar started out by running for office in his residence hall and was elected president of the Hall Council. That was a good way to make linkages across campus with other student leaders, but it also mostly limited him to first- and second-year students.

As Edgar thought about other options, he considered writing for the student newspaper as he had in high school. That would have been lots of fun, but it was also a major time commitment, so he held off on that option. He attended a few meetings of the campus chapter of a national political party, but he was turned off by some of the seniors who were the current officers.

Finally, Edgar decided he would run for campuswide student government office in the spring term election in order to serve in his sophomore year. Student politics, he found, were much more cutthroat in college than they had been in high school, with lots of dirty tricks and nasty personal game playing. Some students didn't like that Edgar was Hispanic, and most just didn't like his ambition and success. After all, they had goals very similar to Edgar's—becoming the top student leaders on campus. Edgar didn't care much for that kind of nastiness, but he was determined to go after his goal and knew it was important to be known on campus. His friends told him he looked more and more stressed out, but Edgar knew that would necessarily come with the territory of political office.

Happily, Edgar was elected in a close race to be one of his school's representatives to the campuswide student government. This was all part of his plan. In this, his first year, he had been elected to two different campus offices. Edgar was starting to be known as one of the young campus leaders, and he was gaining influence and status. College had started very successfully.

What lay ahead for Edgar? He hoped to run for campus president in the next academic year and was looking for internships in Washington, D.C., with his congressman this summer and with his senator the next summer. He would major in political science and go to law school, and his future seemed as bright as possible—Edgar was on his way to becoming the first Hispanic president of the United States.

61 Join Campus Organizations and Participate in Campus Activities

Are you wondering what you'll be doing each day at college with all the free time you have? Are you worried about being bored, that nothing will interest you, that you'll just be sitting in your room wasting away the hours? Then think again.

Outside of studying, which no doubt will take more of your time than you anticipate, there will be more events to attend and activities to participate in than you could ever imagine. Do you even want to try to count the number of student organizations on your campus? Guess a number in the many hundreds. How about the number of activities that will be available to you during your first year of college? For that answer, guess the number of days of the academic year, then multiply by the many tens of activities that take place each day.

One of the biggest problems in getting involved is figuring out how to make sense of all that's going on. How do you access the rich resources of your campus? The campus newspaper is always a good resource to find lists of events, as is the campus information center, often located in the student union. The student union and other campus buildings, including your residence hall, will have bulletin boards covered with posters and announcements of activities. Get in the habit of reading those boards. You should, of course, go online and identify a few key Web sites that are regularly updated and check them frequently. Your living-learning community is a very good pathway to getting involved in campuswide organizations. Friends, professors, and other word-of-mouth sources are probably your best resources—keep talking and listening.

Many campuses have big fairs near the start of school to introduce you to all the organizations on campus. Be sure to put your name and e-mail address on the sign-up lists for any that seem safe and even of moderate interest. Don't be shy about getting on these contact lists. They will allow you to be aware of organizational meetings and of opportunities to get involved. Many campus organizations also have open houses or mass meetings to recruit and welcome new students. Of course, you don't need to wait for organizations to contact you. Don't hesitate to e-mail or call any organization you're even vaguely interested in to find out when they are meeting. Be sure to go to those first meetings to check out the people, the mood, and the activities and opportunities that exist for new members and to see whether the group is a good fit for you.

There are a dizzying array of activities to choose from and get involved in on campus. Don't be overwhelmed by the choices. Try out new activities that you think you'll like and try entirely new possibilities with the expectation that some will appeal to you and others won't. Take your level of involvement one day at a time. Manage your time, stay active, explore the new and the old, enrich and expand your world, and have a terrific college experience.

62 Go to Lectures, Museums, Workshops, Talks, and Concerts

College learning takes place not only in the classroom but outside the classroom as well. If you keep in mind the notion of college as a scholarly community, you will quickly realize that your community is an environment filled with the riches of intellectual, cultural, and social learning. You should take full advantage of all of these aspects of learning in the community.

Every college campus has numerous guest speakers and lectures. People who are world famous as well as those who are brilliant and wonderful but less well known will be visiting your college every year for talks in academic departments and in policy meetings with administrators and faculty. Authors, poets, and artists give wonderful readings and performances.

Most of these visitors love to spend time with students and make themselves available to give talks, have dinner with students, or visit classrooms. Don't miss out on these scholars, political figures, and artists. They will enrich your life and expand your scholarly community.

Student groups also sponsor guest speakers who are well-known public, media, or governmental leaders. This is a great opportunity to see firsthand people you've seen, read, and heard about in the news, in books, or on TV. Seeing them in person will give you a whole new perspective on who they are and what they represent. You will be drawn to some, repulsed by others, and entertained by still others.

Similarly, all kinds of great theater and musical concerts from around the world will be available to you in college, usually at discounted student rates. If you attend college in an urban area, you may find that you have a much wider variety of these enrichment experiences to choose from, but you'll have to travel off campus to attend. It's good to go into the city as much as you can. If you're on a campus that is not in an urban area, then it's more likely that the performances will come to you, but probably there will be fewer choices. In either case, your response should be the same—make a point of attending.

Don't forget all the museums you can visit. Your college or your city will have any number of art and natural science museums to explore. Use these visits as an opportunity to build on what you've learned in your art history, archaeology, and science classes.

The campus will also have numerous different racial, ethnic, religious, and cultural groups. Many of these groups hold special concerts and celebrations that are open to the entire campus. These performances can be spectacular, invigorating, and inspiring for both participating college peers and audience members. Such events are not to be missed.

Attending these lectures, concerts, museums, and performances will broaden your horizons immeasurably. You should develop these habits for your entire life. The truth of the matter is, however, that now is the time to take full advantage of these opportunities because in college you are likely to have more unstructured time, fewer responsibilities for children and parents, and much more deeply discounted tickets than you will have after you leave college.

63 Stay Involved in Campus Life as a Commuter Student

If you commute to campus, there are lots of reasons why it's more difficult for you to be actively involved in campus life, but none of those reasons are good enough to keep you away. You just have to make up your mind that you're going to be actively involved and then follow through on that commitment. It's important for your education, for your connections with faculty and fellow students, and for your personal and social development. It will make a difference in the likelihood of your academic success.

One of the keys to both college satisfaction and success is the degree to which you feel connected or linked to the institution. Feeling connected through academics is the best way to do this, but it's also critical to make these connections through campus-life activities.

A good first way to make campus more than a disparate series of classes and exams is to find a physical space that is your home on campus. It's good to have a sense of place for anything that's important to you. The best way to accomplish this as a commuter student, though it will take some time, is for you to be so involved in a campus organization that you get to use the offices of the organization as a place where you can leave your things, study, and be with people. A second choice is to find a locker or a room on campus where you can safely leave your belongings and where you can return each day you come to campus. In addition to this locker or room, find a couple other locations that you can claim as home. One might be at a friend's campus apartment or a particularly good study space in one of the libraries or coffee shops, or you might want to find a favorite lounge chair or table in the student union near some good eateries.

Some learning communities on commuter campuses have talked about creating special physical spaces for commuter students. The goal of doing so would be to bring the commuter students together into a more cohesive community on campus. Find out if your learning community or college has set aside any space for you, as a commuter student, to create a place for yourself.

As a commuter student, your time is much less flexible than the college campus often expects. Therefore, it is your responsibility to carefully structure your schedule and manage your time. With regard to participating in campus organizations and attending campus events, you will need to be more attentive to scheduling conflicts and time demands than other students. You may want to try to take late classes on certain days so you can also attend events or meetings in the evening while keeping other days free for work and family. As long as you have a secure place to leave your belongings, you will be much more flexible to coordinate your campus days than if you have to carry everything with you each time you come to campus. Ask the organizations you want to participate in to be sensitive to your constraints and to try to work with your schedule, just as you are trying to adapt to theirs. Do your utmost to make these arrangements work.

64 Take Full Advantage of Learning Opportunities as a Commuter Student

If you are a commuter student, will you still have an opportunity to get to know faculty, attend office hours, meet your peers for study groups, hang out after class to discuss class topics, and attend cocurricular lectures, speakers, and political debates? The answer is yes, you will certainly have that opportunity, but you must be assertive to make sure it happens.

One of the best ways to take advantage of all your learning opportunities is to participate in a learning community. The learning community will provide you with a group of students who are eager to engage with one another and build friendships around intellectual ideas and academic projects. It will also introduce you to faculty who seek to mentor and get to know students in a more individual and personal way.

Many faculty hold office hours immediately before or after classes meet. Therefore, you should plan to come to class early or leave later after class in order to meet with your professors during office hours. Build office hour time into your regular commuting schedule rather than having to make all sorts of special travel arrangements when there is a problem at hand and you have no choice but to see your teacher.

Similarly, if your schedule permits, plan on staying on campus later one or two days each week. Campus talks and speakers usually take place late in the afternoon or early evening. Try to leave some designated time in your campus schedule to make your attendance at these events an occasional or even routine occurrence. Study groups will usually take place in the evening, so by leaving an evening free you will be able to participate with your classroom peers in these important study sessions. In addition to focusing on the specific topic at hand, study groups always lend themselves to discussion of a wide range of topics related to your class discussions. These gatherings will give you access to the valuable learning that also takes place in the informal spaces of college when students just hang out together.

It's more difficult but not impossible by any means to be fully involved in the college scholarly community as a commuter student. You just need to be organized at home, at work, and at college and to manage your time effectively. Be sure that your plan as a college student is not to just take courses but to be an engaged learner—engaged with your texts, your professors, and your fellow students. Doing this will increase your satisfaction with your college experience and should benefit your academic success at college.

65 Develop Leadership Skills

One of the goals of higher education is to develop an informed citizenry who will be active participants and leaders in a diverse democracy. You want to emerge from your college education as one of those active participants and leaders.

There are many different types of leaders and many different leadership opportunities. You should consider trying all of them to acquire experience and skills but also to see what fits you best. You have probably already had experience with the traditional model of leadership—a single head of a hierarchically arranged organization.

Living on your residence hall floor over the course of a year, you will be confronted with occasional roommate conflicts, arguments over loud music, inconsiderate and rude behavior, and perhaps even racial or religious insensitivities. Your floor will need a student who emerges as a leader, apart from the resident advisor, who will set the proper moral tone and create an environment in which people learn to talk through differences and disagreements.

In your classes, you can be an intellectual leader. You can do this by coming to class not only prepared (having completed the assignment) but also ready to ask probing questions and offer critical insights about the day's assignments. You can be a good listener and respond appropriately to other students' comments. You can attend faculty office hours. You can help organize study groups and support your fellow students who raise good issues or who come to you with questions.

In addition to hierarchical leadership, some people act as leaders through their ability to collaborate effectively with others. Working effectively in teams is a skill that most people require in all aspects of life, from the office to the community to home. Yet it is an exceedingly difficult skill and one that few people fully master. Finding opportunities to develop this skill through study groups, group papers, lab projects, research projects, and planning events for student organizations will serve you well and give you valuable experience.

Another kind of leadership is that of the boundary-crosser. Purposefully engage in meaningful ways with people and settings that are new to you. You will begin to gain the ability and readiness to cross boundaries not only without fear but with anticipation for the rich learning and growth that emerge from those interactions and associations. Those who can do this well will be highly effective in managing social relations in their social life and in the workplace.

At some colleges you will have an opportunity to demonstrate leadership by serving as a student facilitator of course discussions. Student facilitators lead discussions in service-learning courses, intergroup dialogues, university 101–type courses, and other situations. Taking on this role requires responsibility, organizational skills, good discussion and listening skills, and the ability to assert oneself and intervene when necessary.

Finally, in addition to all of these informal opportunities to develop leadership skills, many colleges offer classes, workshops, and retreats on leadership. In these activities, you will do readings, review case studies, and learn what makes good leaders in all of the different styles where leadership exists and is necessary. Students who participate in these activities tell me that they find them highly informative, empowering, and loads of fun.

SAM ROBBINS—*"I Wish I Didn't Have to Live at Home."*

It was the traffic each morning that Sam Robbins hated the most. It was so hard for him to get out of bed that he always got a late start. Not only did he have to skip breakfast, but he knew that his longtime friend, Jeff, whom he picked up each day, would be complaining about how late he was. He had to hope that there would be no accidents or delays on his route to college, or they would both be late for the start of class.

Sam was doing pretty well in his college classes, but he had a very busy schedule to keep up with. Immediately after class, he rushed off to work for a half-day shift, and then he returned home to study and finish his homework.

Sam accepted the fact that his parents couldn't afford to pay for his college education, and he understood that even if he worked full time he wouldn't be able to pay both tuition and room and board. With his half-time job and full-time summer work, he was going to get by with only a minimum of loans, and he was very thankful for that.

Sam didn't mind being busy or working, but he still wasn't too happy about his overall existence. Most of Sam's friends had gone away to college—either attending college out of state or attending college in town but living on campus. They all told him about the fun times they were having on campus, going to parties, hanging out together late at night, meeting new people, and experiencing all kinds of new things.

Sam wouldn't admit to being jealous, but he knew he wasn't having loads of fun. His parents tried to be nice to him and give him his independence, but he had had enough of living with them. He wanted his own place. Conversely, sometimes he thought his friends were a bit spoiled, just spending all their families' money to party and "grow up." He felt good about the job he had and about how people respected him for his good work ethic.

College was okay, too, but it felt like high school. Classes were more chal-
lenging, but he didn't feel any school spirit. He didn't have time to meet new
people or participate in campus activities. He couldn't even go to the study
groups because they met at night, and it was a big hassle to drive back to cam-
pus after work.

One day, a professor assigned a project that required small groups of students
to meet outside of class. Sam spoke up in class to complain that he had to work
after class each day. His professor was sympathetic, but rather than excuse Sam
from the assignment, he suggested a number of ways that the group could accom-
modate Sam's schedule.

Sam agreed to drive back to campus for a few nights over the next two weeks
to meet with his small group. Although he was very annoyed at first, he slowly
began to see some advantages to being on campus at night. He couldn't help but
notice how lively the campus was, and he was amazed at how much fun it
seemed to be. At first, that made him feel even worse for himself, but after a
couple of his group meetings, his classmates invited him to hang out with them
afterward. All of a sudden, he had begun to make his first college friends. He
loved the fact that he had new friends, and he also realized that he felt more pos-
itively about the college overall.

When the project was done, Sam was really happy with the time he had spent
on campus and the new friends he had made. However, he was saddened to
think he was going to return to his routine of class, work, and homework at his
parents' home. He talked to one of his new friends, who suggested matter-of-factly
that Sam join him on an intramural basketball team. Sam loved basketball, and
though it was a long drive just to play ball, he decided to give it a try.

Sam joined the team and came to campus once a week for games. At least
some of the guys on the team usually went out to eat after the games, and Sam
started sticking around for the after-game fun. By doing this, he began to meet
other students and got some ideas for other activities he could get involved with

on campus. He would check the student newspaper for lectures and special events that were taking place the night he was on campus.

With his busy schedule, his life began to get very full, but at least now his motivation was much higher, and he found he was able to get his homework done much more quickly than in the past. True, he walked around tired much of the time. But Sam's school spirit rose dramatically, as did his commitment to his studies. He liked having friends at college, and he began to feel like a full-fledged member of his campus. It made a big difference to Sam's experience as a college student.

66   Explore Religion, Spirituality, and a Life of Commitment

In a society so focused on wealth and material goods, many students today are looking for something more meaningful in their lives. Some are looking for the comfort, faith, and solace of a god or religion to help them make sense of the world, while others are searching for answers in spirituality or a spiritual community.

You may identify closely with a particular religion when you arrive at college, or you may be less closely affiliated with an organized religion but still want to find deeper meaning and commitments in your life. This interest in organized religion or a search for spirituality is increasingly true of students who are attending college today.

There are many religious-affiliated campus organizations on most campuses. These organizations seek to provide a campus center for you in the denomination of your religious faith that you followed at home. They are student centered, and they usually offer both religious and social activities to encourage your continued involvement and pursuit of religion while in college with a group of peers from the same faith.

Many other students either object to organized religions or have found that they do not provide the spiritual foundation and grounding they are seeking. These students may discover what they are looking for, transcending the formalities of religious practice and organized religions, in books, nature, friendships, and meaningful connections with like-minded people who are searching for something deeper in life.

Some students try to convert other students to join a different religion or to follow a particular religious or spiritual path they have chosen for themselves. I don't know of any students who have appreciated being proselytized on college campuses by their fellow students.

Over the years, some groups have periodically misrepresented their mission and preyed on college students, attempting to recruit impressionable college students to join cults. I still remember being approached by followers of such a group, on my first day on campus prior to attending graduate school classes at the University of California at Berkeley. A couple of welcoming young people, without any mention of their religious group, asked me to come join them at their house for what they described as "a festive dinner with a group of friendly students," an opportunity to meet people in my new town. As a graduate student, I knew what their dangerous ploy was all about, but it was certainly slick and deceptive, and a first-year college student would have been hard-pressed to turn them down. Be forewarned about groups that misrepresent their intentions.

These searches for faith, religion, spirituality, and meaning in life are likely to be of great importance to you, just as they have been to generations of humans seeking to understand the mysteries and the commonplace of our lives. Use the many resources available on campus and surrounding your campus. Consult with many peers and elders, but don't just follow what other folks, both the well meaning and the untrustworthy, tell you to do or believe. Find your own answers and path. Be smart and thoughtful about this and take your time on this important journey.

67 Consider Whether Fraternities and Sororities Are for You

Your decision as to whether or not to join a fraternity or sorority can have a big impact on how you experience college.

The myths and stereotypes of fraternities and sororities, both good and bad, are legendary and extreme. The truth is that there are many different types of fraternities and sororities on every college campus, some resembling the best and some the very worst of the stereotypes, with many falling closer to the middle. In most cases, however, they do represent a significant investment of time, money, and emotional commitment. Therefore, you should make this choice carefully and deliberately.

Fraternities and sororities have a number of different organizational foci. Find out what types of organizations exist on your campus and what percentage of students participate.

The majority are social organizations, with an emphasis on group bonding, social cohesion, and social activities to bring the membership together. There are also a smaller number that have service as their primary focus, providing educational support or tutoring to students on campus and sometimes in the community. An even smaller number come together for religious fellowship.

Most fraternities and sororities belong to the national umbrella groups, the Interfraternity Conference or Panhellenic Conference. While these organizations are open to all students, individual houses are predominantly and sometimes exclusively white and heterosexual, and many tend to be religiously homogeneous. Similarly, the Black Greek Association includes fraternities and sororities that tend to be exclusively Black. In recent years, there have emerged a growing number of independent fraternities and sororities that are Latino, Asian American, gay/lesbian, or intentionally multiethnic.

The great appeal of these organizations, of course, is the strong friendships that evolve over time, in some cases lasting for a lifetime. However, those friendships grow, in part, because of the intensity of the group activities coupled with the very demanding time commitments required of new pledges and members.

Those nonacademic time commitments, particularly during the first semester of college, create critical academic problems for a certain number of students each year.

In response to the downsides of the time commitment and the staging of rush activities right when students enter college, a growing number of fraternities and sororities are moving rush to the second semester or second year of college, as is the practice of the Black Greek Association. Timing is one of the things you should consider when deciding whether and when to rush a fraternity or sorority.

The continuing homogeneity of fraternities and sororities is another important consideration. On many campuses, students in fraternities and sororities, particularly white students on predominantly white campuses, are among the most isolated on campus in terms of social diversity. Diversity is an important part of your education and growth in college, so you should consider how well you will be able to address that value of college if you join a fraternity or sorority that is both homogeneous and very demanding of your time and attention.

The final consideration is the behavior of the overall Greek system on your campus and the student members who are in the individual fraternities or sororities you would consider rushing. Fit is everything here. To what extent does the culture of the sorority or fraternity you wish to rush match your values in terms of academic achievement, social relationships, alcohol use, diversity, and respect for self and others. It's a good time to examine what you hope to gain from your college education and to consider to what extent fraternity/sorority life will enhance or detract from your goals.

Don't rush your decision about rush. Make a careful, thoughtful choice that will be best for you.

68 Get Around Town without a Car

A significant number of students coming to college have had access to cars—either their parents' cars or their own—while in high school. Yet most colleges, except, of course, for commuter campuses, require or advise students not to bring cars to college, especially during the first year. You might be wondering how you're going to manage without one or even whether you should try to ignore your college's advice and bring one anyway.

The reason for college rules about cars is the lack of parking on college campuses. Whether your college is an urban campus or is in a small town or rural area, parking is at a premium. One of the most common themes across college campuses is the universal complaining—not only by students but even more so by faculty and staff—about the high cost and limited availability of parking spaces. Everyone's unhappy.

The best way to get your mind around the no-car problem is to think of this as a liberating opportunity rather than as a burden or punishment. If you're attending an urban college, then hopefully your city has a great public transportation system.

Many other campuses are relatively self-contained or are located in small towns or cities. Restaurants, shopping, movies, concerts, and so forth are all within walking distance of your residence hall room. You will love the freedom of walking or bicycling to where you need to go. It's good exercise, invigorating, energizing, healthy, and much more social than riding alone in your car.

There are times, however, when you will really need or want a car to get off campus. What will you do in these situations?

Fortunately, there are some relatively easy answers to these problems in most cases. Some more isolated campuses provide shuttle buses for students to go to places of high demand, such as a mall or a metro stop. At peak travel and vacation times, most campuses have private or public transportation available for students to get to the airport or train station. Almost all campuses that are not near public transit provide students with van or car transportation to community service-learning locations.

Finally, even when your campus lacks a first-rate metro system, most towns have limited bus and taxi service. Learn to use the local bus system. And learn to pedal—bikes are great modes of transportation—just remember to wear a helmet.

Not having a car saves a lot of money, too. You won't have to make car payments or pay for gas or insurance. It also saves the environment. All the pollutants emitted by cars are reduced by each of the thousands of students who have had to leave cars at home while they are in college. So you're not only doing yourself a financial favor, you're also helping to save the planet!

Health and Safety

69 Live a Well-Rounded Life

You want to grow and develop as a whole person in college. In order to do this, you need to find ways to be a well-rounded person who takes advantage of the wide range of opportunities available in college.

Academics are at the center of a college education. Achieving academic success, in terms of mastery of academic content, skills, and processes, is a critical goal. Developing as an adult and learning how you can best make a difference in the world as an educated individual is a necessity. Learning skills in problem solving, building relationships, and managing conflicts are essential.

To accomplish all of these important goals in college, you will need to find balance in your life. You want to begin modeling a healthy, balanced lifestyle that you can sustain throughout your life.

Your challenge during college is to succeed academically but at the same time to allow yourself to grow and blossom in many aspects of your life. To do this, you will need to learn to effectively manage your time and make difficult choices.

You will find you have to spend more time studying in college than in high school. You will have so much unstructured time that you will find yourself staying up late but wondering where all the hours of the day went. You will be thrilled with all the wonderful opportunities to learn and participate outside the classroom, but in order to keep your head in the books, you'll have to learn to sometimes say no to those activities and to good friends. And, for some students, the opposite will be the case. You'll have to learn to say yes to go out, to be with friends and do things outside of the classroom, and to get your head out of the books.

Some students talk about a lifestyle whereby they "study hard and party hard." That works for some, but I'm not sure that's the best approach either. I think it can lead to a binge mentality that leads to extremes, like workaholic and alcoholic tendencies. I advocate lightening up a bit on yourself and developing a lifestyle that you can sustain over your lifetime.

Live a balanced and well-rounded life. Learn to enjoy your studies, enjoy learning, enjoy your time with friends, and love life itself.

70 Take Care of Your Soul

As much as your mind and your physical body need your care, attention, and stimulation, so does your inner soul. Feed and nurture it, and you will be that much stronger and more grounded to face each day.

Beyond any material goals or even academic achievements, what is important to you in life? What are your values? When you get down to the essentials in your life, what matters most? What keeps you going each day? What is your purpose in life?

You will know if you are having academic troubles in your classes because your professor will speak to you or you will find yourself getting grades that are below your expectations or are simply not passing. Your mind will let you know whether you are stimulated by your teachers and by the related intellectual content of the courses. Your body will tell you if you are not feeling well or if you have sustained an injury.

It's just as important to have some mechanisms to keep track of whether your soul is healthy or aching. Do people speak well of you, the person, not just of your accomplishments or the clothes you wear? Do your friends like you because of your generous spirit, or do they like you because you own a car or have a new TV in your room? Do you like yourself because of your good looks, because of awards you have received, or because you like what you stand for in the world?

Do you feel good about who you are? Do you not only like the personality you present to others but also like the person inside whom you know better than anyone else? Can you not only live with yourself but also appreciate and respect who you are?

You may want to determine what things nurture your soul. It might be a good friendship. It might be good family relationships. You could be heartened by the story of someone's life that you read about in a book or watch in a movie. Perhaps you feel good after doing something good for another person, for your community, or for an animal or for the environment. You might need to learn something new and inspiring, appreciate a work of art or music, or gain insight into something you never understood before. Your soul might be nurtured by your connection with your faith or god or by appreciating the bounty of the earth when you eat some fresh fruit and vegetables. You might get this feeling from a deeply moving conversation with a friend, a teacher, a parent, or grandparent or from the joy of holding a newborn baby.

Being healthy has many dimensions. Be sure you take care of your body and mind, but be just as concerned with your essence, your soul.

71 Get Away from Campus during the Semester

College is a world unto itself. It has its own unique and wondrous culture, and it requires you to invest a lot of your personal and intellectual time and energy in it. It is often an intense emotional experience and usually a very good one.

It is necessary sometimes to take a step back from intense experiences. At college that means getting away on occasion, even if for just an hour, a day, or a weekend.

Getting away might mean a visit home, but it often can mean many other things. Getting away could mean going out of town to a concert, theater, or sporting event. It could mean going shopping at a nearby mall, close enough that it's easy to quickly get to but far enough away that you need to take a bus, subway, or car. Sometimes all you need is a walk in the park or going out to see a movie, in the sense that getting away means more a mental break than a significant physical separation. It might even mean taking a good, refreshing break from your studies by buying an ice cream cone or taking a yoga class.

For some college students, what is needed is a break from other people. They spend so much intense time together with a group of friends, especially students living in a residence hall, that getting away means spending time with a different group of people. You might need to do this by visiting friends living at home or at a different college, but it also might mean just finding friends in other social circles on campus. It might mean spending time by yourself, either being contemplative or doing some other familiar activity to get back in touch with your special needs and individuality.

I recommend getting away in any of the senses above at least a couple times a month. I also think it's good to physically get away from campus at least once per month.

Getting away should be restorative, and you should not wait until you feel you have to run away from something bad. Take this break when you feel strong and good. Use it as preventative medicine and health care.

If you are wise about your time away, then you will come back to all the things you love about college all the more ready to rejoin the intense community and cultural experience. Your body will be renewed and your mind cleared of cobwebs cluttering much needed space to explore and take in all the good new learning that is taking place. Your friends will appreciate you more, you will do better in your work, and you will be happier with yourself.

—

LAUREN GOLDSTEIN—*"Turn the Page on Today's Disaster."*

For Lauren Goldstein, it was one of those days when just everything seemed to go wrong. It was the fourth week of college. Everything had been going smoothly. Classes were challenging, but Lauren was keeping up and getting As and Bs on her papers and quizzes. Lauren had met many people and had found some girls on her floor that she could see herself getting close to.

Bobby had called late the night before. They got into a fight over the phone, and Lauren knew it was the end of the relationship. Bobby was talking about wanting to meet new people. Lauren was hurt and angry, but she didn't let on.

She wasn't ready to give up on her relationship with her high school steady boyfriend, even though it was such a strain to try to maintain a long-distance relationship when there was so much new in her life at college. Still, Bobby persisted in the idea until Lauren finally caved in and tearily said they should take a break from one another and try seeing others.

Lauren cried all night and didn't get to sleep till very late—so late, in fact, that she slept through her nine o'clock anthropology class. She skipped breakfast and ran across campus to her ten o'clock calculus class to take her first real test of the semester. She left the class shaking because she felt she had done so poorly. Many of her classmates were complaining that the test was unfair, that there were trick questions, and that the homework problem sets hadn't prepared them for the questions asked. The professor did not seem sympathetic.

Lauren came back to the residence hall for lunch and could barely eat. Her friends tried to cheer her up. She missed her parents and wanted to talk with them about Bobby, but she also didn't want to tell them how badly she had done on her test. She was tired and hungry and hurting inside.

After lunch Lauren went to her history seminar, her favorite class. She hardly said a word, and when the professor questioned her about one of the readings, she said something off the point and rambled along until another student interrupted. She could tell—or at least she imagined it was so—that the professor gave her a disparaging look. She knew she had sounded utterly stupid!

She decided to skip her next class and go back to her room but got soaked walking across campus in the rain. It had been a long, miserable day. Time moved so slowly. The minutes crept by. Lauren wondered what she was going to do. Maybe she had made a mistake; maybe she should transfer to a school back home.

At dinner, Jacob came over and sat next to her. Lauren really liked Jacob but hadn't let herself get close to him while she was involved with Bobby. Jacob was funny and easy to be with. He didn't make any demands on Lauren and listened to her when she spoke. Sallie, who was the silliest and nicest girl she had ever met, came over to sit with Lauren and Jacob and jumped in with the craziest and funniest story Lauren had ever heard. The story made no sense at all, but the three of them couldn't help but laugh out loud all through dinner. On the way out of the cafeteria, Sallie remembered she had picked up Lauren's paper from the English class she had skipped. Her professor wrote on the back page of her paper, "Lauren—this is the best writing you've done this term. Your story is thoughtful, analytical and clearly written! Great Work! A."

A few hours later, Lauren was up late studying and preparing for the next day's classes. The phone rang, and it was her mom. She had already heard that Lauren and Bobby had broken up and was worried that Lauren might be taking it hard. "Oh that," Lauren said, "I was so upset at first, but I'm moving on. I think I'm ready to meet some new guys here. It is a big deal, but not that big of a deal."

Lauren hung up the phone and wondered why her mother seemed so concerned. Things were looking up at college. Sure, things wouldn't always go perfectly, but she was an adult now, and the breakup with Bobby had happened so long ago. Life was moving forward so fast and intensely at college that there was little time to be stuck. That had all happened so long ago—well, it certainly seemed longer than twenty-four hours ago!

Tonight Lauren was thinking about Jacob, Sallie, her strong writing skills, and getting ready for her next calculus exam.

72 Go to Sleep If You're Tired

"Don't get mono." That straightforward piece of advice comes directly from one of my favorite students. Mononucleosis should be avoided, of course. But many students get so busy with their lives that they push and push their bodies to their limit and beyond. Then, when they get mono, they are surprised that they had forgotten the straightforward advice of my wise student.

My student's advice speaks about much more than mono, however. It's all about looking after the health of your body. Feed it and sleep it and it will be there for you to fully enjoy all those wonderful, electrifying moments of college life. It will sustain you through some of the more difficult and stressful times as well. Ignore your body, and even though you probably won't get mono, you'll still have colds, be sluggish, and won't be able to participate at 100+% to do everything you want at college.

Don't forget to sleep. Pretty simple advice, right? The truth is that too many students get very little sleep on a regular basis and more than a few skip sleeping entirely, more than anyone would like to think.

It's a myth that students don't go to bed in college before two in the morning or that no one starts studying till after eleven at night. Some few students do study well after things quiet down in the wee hours of the night, but most students' academic productivity and retention decreases dramatically once they get tired. This is not rocket science.

Though eating and sleeping are things you've done your entire life, in a funny way, they are new experiences at college. Cafeteria food presents great opportunities, such as plentiful food and no need for cooking and washing dishes. It also presents new challenges that may lead you to eat more than you ever wanted or less than you really need.

You may have heard about the "freshman fifteen." I think you should just follow the sound dietary advice given to everyone, either in or out of college, that you should do your best to eat healthy foods and exercise regularly. Yes, you may gain a few pounds or lose a few pounds due to all the changes when you first start college, but if you're exercising and generally making healthy choices from the array of foods in the cafeteria, you'll do just fine.

What you should concern yourself with is keeping a positive attitude and a good sense of self-esteem. It's much easier to do so when your body is getting nourished.

Don't forget to eat. Some students get so involved at exam time or during their involvement in some major campus activity that they skip meals, thinking they can get by till the next mealtime comes along. If you miss meals, you'll feel weaker, be more stressed, have less internal stamina to constructively manage all the activities in your life, and be more vulnerable to getting sick.

Don't forget to dress appropriately for the weather. If it's raining, don't worry first about fashion. Bring an umbrella or wear a raincoat. You don't want to be walking around campus soaked all day. If it's cold and snowing, don't go out in a T-shirt and shorts. Wear heavy socks, a sweater, gloves, scarf, heavy coat, hat, and some good boots. Think about thermal underwear. It's more fashionable to be healthy and participating in everything than lying in bed with a fever.

And what about when you're starting to feel a little under the weather? Again, listen to your body. If your throat is sore, drink some hot tea or orange juice and eat a bowl of chicken soup. If you're cold and it's snowing outside, dress warmly. If you're more tired than usual, get extra sleep.

You're in college—you're smart and you know all this advice. Practice it in college, and your body will thank you by working at full efficiency.

73 Exercise and Play Sports

Regular exercise is good for your physical and mental health. Moving to college from high school will require you to adapt new routines and find new means to get your body moving, but be sure to keep active.

Most campuses have state-of-the-art recreational facilities, including all manner of strength and exercise machines, tracks, swimming pools, and courts for basketball, handball, and racquetball. They offer exercise classes from traditional stretching to the latest training regimens.

Many students enjoy running with friends on trails throughout the campus and on the city streets. It's a great way to be with people, get to know your way around town, stay in shape, and feel good about yourself. There are always fun and competitive races, some for pleasure and some to raise funds for good causes.

Sports and college go hand in hand. It can be great fun watching big-time intercollegiate competitions, but there are opportunities to play on competitive intramural sports teams in almost any sport imaginable. Football, basketball, volleyball, field hockey, soccer, ultimate Frisbee, golf, and skiing are just a few of the sports in which students participate. On most campuses you can choose teams that are coed, all-male, or all-female, and you can also choose to be in leagues that are more or less competitive.

Team sports are a good way to meet people, build your skills, have fun, and learn to work collaboratively with others. They are a good break from your academic focus and can give you a regular activity to look forward to and provide structure to your free time. Make sure you pick a team that you like and a sport that you enjoy. Your team sport should be fun for you, not an additional stress in your life.

By exercising your body, you will feel renewed, and you will find that your mind is refreshed as well. You will come back from exercise with some new and probably more constructive insights about conflicts you are facing, problems you need to solve, studying you need to do, and tasks you need to accomplish. It will help to reduce the clutter in your mind and allow you to move more happily and productively through your day.

74 Limit Your All-Nighters

It's not true that you must pull all-nighters to consider yourself an authentic college student.

All-nighters are not a good idea generally and certainly not a good habit to get into. Most students' attention spans and ability to focus decrease rapidly as they get tired. You are fooling yourself if you think your ability to study and retain knowledge will be effective after you become tired.

This is college, after all, and the work is difficult, complex, and challenging—even when you're at your most alert. Unfortunately, *alert* would not be the word to describe most students at four in the morning.

Rather than studying ahead of time, some students resort to drinking cup after cup of coffee to keep themselves alert and awake throughout the night. The results can be pretty ugly the day after. When you're actually taking the history exam or giving your Spanish speech at eleven, your coffee withdrawal will hit you hard, complete exhaustion will take over your body, and your mind will go limp. It's just not a winning strategy.

Worse than coffee is that some students resort to taking speed or over-the-counter medications to keep them alert through the night. This is truly a disaster in the making. The fact that you are resorting to drug stimulants for the sake of writing a paper or studying for an exam should serve as a wake-up call to you. At a minimum it's a sign that your perspective on things has become badly distorted.

If you find that you are pulling more than one all-nighter per month, you should consider going to your academic counselor to find help with study and time management skills. If you're using any controlled substances, go to health services and your counseling office immediately for confidential advice, medical attention, and support.

Remember, you're in college because you're smart, motivated, and a good student. In high school you probably complained that school should start later because you needed more hours of sleep. In college you still need your sleep. You need to sleep to remain alert and up to the challenges of college. Be smart about your study skills, time management, and physical and mental health.

75 Be Safe in Sex

Whether you're a man or a woman, straight or gay, you need to become educated about safe sex. If you don't know how to protect yourself and your prospective partner before you come to college, take the first days of college to get a crash course on the subject. You and your prospective partner's health and life depend on it.

As an adult, you will make your own decisions about whether or not to have sexual relations during your college years. The fact is, however, that large numbers of college students are sexually active and do engage in intercourse, and those who do, as well as their friends, need to know what to do to avoid unwanted pregnancy and sexually transmitted diseases.

Sexual choices are serious ones, with personal, emotional, social, and religious ramifications. Too many students are too skittish to talk about sexual relations and sex education, even though they've been exposed to TV shows, music videos, talk shows, and movies that seem totally consumed with sex. The consequences of unprotected sex can leave you with enduring and dangerous illnesses such as HIV/AIDS, unwanted pregnancies, and difficult personal choices about abortion or raising a child.

One of the best ways that sexually active people can avoid having unsafe sex is to remain sober. All kinds of bad judgments and ill-considered actions take place under the influence of alcohol. The likelihood of having unwanted and unprotected sex rises exponentially if you are under the influence of alcohol or other drugs.

What are some places and times to be particularly on guard for the mix of alcohol and (unprotected) sex? The first days of college, before classes start, are notorious for parties with heavy drinking and upperclassmen taking advantage of first-year female students. Pregame and postgame football parties are another time to stay sober if you don't want to get into sexual trouble. Finally, students continue to tell me that some fraternities, despite annual pledges of restraint in alcohol use, remain bastions of out-of-control drinking and unwanted and unprotected sex. Beware!

Another way that sexually active people can avoid unprotected sex is to talk with their steady partners about safe sex. Be sure that both of you are committed to using protection and being safe every time you engage in sexual activity.

Go to health services and talk to a doctor, nurse, or peer health educator to learn what to do to protect yourself. Create an informal support network of friends, female and male alike, to make sure everyone in your group is well educated and has all the protective devices available.

One of my students was a varsity college football player who one year was doing community service with an organization responsible for educational outreach about HIV/AIDS. During the course of his training and subsequent educational outreach work, his awareness and concern about safe sex increased dramatically. One day he came to office hours to tell me that he realized that many of his teammates were putting themselves and their partners in jeopardy because they were so poorly educated about safe sex and because so little protection was being used. He told me that he had begun distributing condoms to the football team and asking around to see if there was interest in more education.

You should follow this student's lead. Get educated. Get condoms and other protection for safe sex. Think about these issues now, well before you find yourself in a situation when it will be that much harder to start the discussion. Find friends who care enough about you and each other to support one another to always be protected and prepared. This is everyone's responsibility: yours, your partner's, and your friends—men and women alike.

76 Control Your Alcohol Use and Don't Use Drugs

You're on your own at college. With regard to alcohol and drug use, you will be able to do pretty much whatever you choose. It is, therefore, important that you give some thought to your use of alcohol and other drugs so you make the choice that is right for you.

The question of how you want to behave in college with regard to alcohol and other drugs is not one you can avoid. Alcohol and drugs will be widely available, and there will be both friendly encouragement and sometimes pressure from friends and social organizations to drink and use drugs. In the residence halls, students you know and like will be inviting you into their rooms to drink, smoke marijuana, or try other drugs. Many off-campus parties will have alcohol and marijuana available for you to use, and many will have other substances available for you to get high.

Come to college having given some thought about how you want to act. You will be able to say yes or no as often as you want. Whether you choose to drink or not will have no impact on your involvement in most college social activities. Most of your peers will be very accepting of your decision not to drink with them, but you will need to have enough self-confidence to say no when the offer presents itself. You may also decide you want to say yes to a few drinks but also later to say no before you've had too much alcohol.

One key issue to think about is why you want to drink or use drugs. If it's because you can't feel relaxed or sociable without a few drinks in you, then maybe those social feelings are something you want to work on without the crutch of a drink. If you think your life is too boring and humdrum, that you can't experience the highs of life that others seem to have without getting high on drugs, maybe you need to examine your life so that you can experience the real joys of living when you're not drinking or using drugs.

Data on binge drinking on college campuses are now collected each year with little variation in the high rates of bingeing. Every year, news reports tell of college students taken to the hospital as a result of alcohol poisoning. Despite the clever and entertaining TV and print ads glamorizing alcohol use, most people know from personal experience that people who are drunk can be gross, destructive, belligerent, and even violent. And the deadly statistics of drinking and driving as well as the dangers of alcohol and drug addiction are all well known. Finally, it's important to keep in mind state laws regarding age requirements, using a fake driver's license as identification, and possessing or selling illegal substances.

Your use of alcohol and other drugs in college is just one more decision you will need to make as a young adult. It will be your decision, not your parents', your teachers', your clergy's, or your friends'. It's ultimately a decision about your mental, emotional, and physical health. Understanding why, whether, and how much you choose to use alcohol or drugs will help you discover more about the life you lead, about the degree of happiness and fulfillment in your life, and what changes you might want to consider making about your very essence. These are important decisions for you as you grow and learn as a bright, independent adult. Choose wisely.

77 Lock Your Door and Don't Walk Home Alone at Night

The simple suggestions to remember to lock your door and never to walk home alone after dark aren't 100% fail-safe, but they're easy, commonsense approaches to personal safety. You ignore them at your own risk.

Most colleges, even those campuses in areas with higher crime rates, have a feeling of safety. Colleges tend to be nurturing, safe environments, with teachers, counselors, peer advisors, and friends all looking out for you. You can easily get the feeling that the worst that could befall you is a bad grade on a test or a bureaucratic person in the registrar's office who keeps you waiting in line and won't give you what you want.

Add to that your own sense of invulnerability that is commonplace with late teens and young adults. You're Superman, Spider-Man, and Wonder Woman all wrapped up in one.

Unfortunately, the ugly, cruel realities of life are right at the doorstep of your college campus. There are crimes of opportunity, crimes of spontaneity, and crime gangs at work. Criminals know when students move into the residence halls. Criminals know that students bring computers, TVs, stereos, and cash. They also know that students will let anyone into their residence hall and that many don't lock their doors.

If you're a criminal, or even another student who wants some good "stuff," it's easy enough to dash into a student room, grab a laptop or wallet off of a desk, and then walk down the hallway looking like any other student. It could happen in the two minutes you go next door to your neighbor's room, or it could happen in the twenty minutes that you go down to the bathroom to take a shower and brush your teeth in the morning.

Some brazen thieves will even walk into your unlocked residence hall rooms late at night while you are asleep to rob you. This doesn't happen frequently, but why risk it? All you need to do is be diligent about locking your door.

The other high crime moment is on the street after dark, particularly late at night. If you're alone on the street late at night, you're asking for trouble, whether you're a man or a woman. If you're a woman, there's also the greater likelihood that you may be the victim of a sexual assault.

Colleges have programs to warn you about these dangers and what precautions to take to be safe. They will tell you to lock your doors at all times and never to walk alone at night. Many campuses have late-night shuttle buses to take you back to your residence hall or even permit you to call campus police for a ride home. There are organized "safe-walk" programs, where you can call for a person to walk you home from late-night studying or partying. Most colleges today have emergency phones throughout the campus that connect directly to the campus police and immediately notify the police of your location.

Respect yourself enough not to let yourself get into dangerous situations. Take simple steps to minimize the odds of becoming a crime victim. Enjoy the freedom of adult independence by being smart enough to use good sense about your safety.

SYLVIA RODRIGUEZ — *"No, Thanks. I'll Pass on That."*
It was her first week of college—actually the week prior to the start of classes—and Sylvia Rodriguez was standing in a frat house with a drink in her hand at about two in the morning. Sylvia had come to college eager to jump into

everything. She was looking forward to meeting her roommates, ready to get in-volved in campus activities, and excited about starting her courses.

She moved into her residence hall about ten days prior to the start of class for a busy week of activities. Sylvia went to all the events of the week, including re-treats, advising workshops, book discussions with faculty, ice cream socials, and loads of late-night parties with lots and lots of alcohol. Her college offered non-alcoholic alternative activities each night, which were fun and well organized, but they weren't truly an alternative because they all ended just around the time the student drinking parties began.

Sylvia loved these activities except for the fact that she hadn't really wanted to go to the late-night parties. Sylvia had grown up learning to have fun and being involved without drinking as part of the fun. Her parents were strict about this, and she agreed with them, so in high school she had just decided not to hang out with those students who chose to drink.

She thought college would be different. Sylvia hadn't expected the social scene to include so much drinking. However, her new friends in the residence hall didn't seem to have any problem with all the drinking, and they tried to convince her to come along. Since Sylvia hadn't made friends yet, she didn't want to be left out, and so one night she decided to go out with the students from her floor.

When she arrived at the party, Sylvia was overwhelmed with the number of people there. It was a body pack. Everyone had a drink in their hands, and the guys seemed to be hitting on all the first-year women. There were kegs and punch bowls everywhere. The music was blaring, and people seemed to be having a good time.

Sylvia and the women from her floor wandered through the crowd to check out the scene. A few of the women immediately got cups of beer and began to get into the mood of the party. They invited Sylvia to join them, but she declined. Some guys came over, introduced themselves, and started talking and laughing with Sylvia's group.

This wasn't Sylvia's type of party, but she had come along and she wanted to fit in and give it a chance. She decided to take a drink after all so at least she looked like part of the party. She acted sociable, met some new guys, and introduced herself to some new women. Like most of her interactions during the week, Sylvia liked some of the people she met but did not like others so much, especially the one guy who kept trying to kiss her.

Despite giving it a try, Sylvia was very uncomfortable. She didn't object to other people drinking, but she did object to herself drinking. The whole scene just wasn't for her. This wasn't how she liked to meet and get to know people. Instead of feeling fun and relaxed at the party, she felt tense and awkward.

Sylvia was very upset but mostly with herself. She had always prided herself on being a strong and independent person, and she felt that she hadn't been that person tonight. Here she was at this party, which wasn't her kind of party, acting in a way that wasn't true to herself. "Okay," she thought, "maybe I'm being too tough on myself. It's good that I gave this a try and took a chance to see if I would like this kind of college party. But, why am I still here? And why am I holding a cup of beer when I don't like beer?"

Sylvia decided to leave the party. A couple of the women from the floor saw her getting ready to leave and joined her right away. The others stayed. On the way home, they realized that they had all felt uncomfortable at the party. As they began to relax, they started talking and sharing with each other about who they really were and what they really liked. They decided to stop for pizza on the way home and made it back to the residence hall by four in the morning.

All in all, Sylvia felt pretty good about the night. She had made some good friends and learned about campus life. Mostly, she had learned a lot about herself. She had made some mistakes, but she had also reaffirmed what she believed in and what kind of person she wanted to be. Classes hadn't even started, but she had already begun her college education.

78 Know How to Get Out of Dangerous Situations

The first rule of safety is that you should not put yourself in a situation that has a high potential to endanger you and others. If you don't do drugs, don't hang out with drug users or dealers. If you want to get home safely late at night, don't walk alone and don't go down dark streets. If you are sexually active but don't want to get sexually transmitted diseases, carefully protect yourself and have safe sex. If you don't want your room to be robbed, lock your door. If you don't want to cause a disastrous car accident, don't drink and drive.

The second rule of safety is to have an exit strategy if you should find yourself in a difficult or dangerous situation. Why do you need this second rule if you follow the first rule? The reason is that you can't always fully control your circumstances, try as you might. Sometimes, through no fault of your own, you will find yourself in a potentially dangerous situation.

Picture yourself going to the library one night to study for an important exam. While you don't plan to stay there very long, you find you are doing good, focused work, and before you know it, it's two in the morning and the library is closing. You quickly gather your belongings and start heading back to your residence hall. Although you've used the campus safe-walk program in the past, this time you're tired and still thinking about the exam questions, and you just start walking across campus. As you walk along, you hear some people shouting things at you. You look back and see a couple of guys you don't recognize and who don't seem friendly. You look around some more and notice that you are the only student walking along this path. Fortunately, you have made a point of knowing where campus emergency phones are located. You know there are several phones on this path, so you hurry to the next one, stop at the phone, and make a quick 911 call. The campus police arrive in less than a minute.

You go to an off-campus party with a friend. You hear that there will be great music and dancing, and your friend encourages you to come along. He has a car, so you ride with him to see his old high school buddies. At first the party is great fun. Before too long, however, everyone starts getting high. You're not particularly comfortable with everyone using drugs, but you try to enjoy the music. As it gets later, you realize that your friend is in no condition to drive safely back to campus. You offer to drive your friend's car, but he doesn't want to leave. Fortunately, you've planned ahead for this kind of situation. You have a cell phone for emergencies, and you carry extra money with you in case you ever need to take a taxi home. You call a taxi, and despite some uncomfortable waiting around, the taxi finally arrives and takes you back to campus.

You've been getting closer to someone you feel very attracted to. The relationship has been great in all respects, and it has not been a sexual relationship. One night you find yourself alone with this person in your residence hall room. Things move along fast—faster than you would have anticipated. You and your friend are about to make love, but you both realize that you don't have any protection. Fortunately, you've talked with friends about what you would do in this situation, so you know how you must act. Despite your desires and despite your concern that this might harm this new relationship, you firmly tell your friend that you won't have sex without protection. Your friend, to your delight, not only agrees with you but expresses relief that you stopped things before you engaged in unprotected sexual intercourse.

These kinds of scenarios or others like them do not happen frequently on campus, but they will happen. You'll be wise to recall situations you've been in where you could have used a good exit strategy and also to imagine possible scenarios in which you'll need a quick response to protect yourself. Be smart, not passive or frightened. It's just one more way to stay safe and healthy in college.

79 Get Help in Case of Emergencies

Despite all your precautions, it is possible that an emergency situation may occur during the several years that you're in college. When you lived at home, you might have depended on your parent(s) to respond in the event of emergencies. Now you should be prepared to do so, and by all means you should take action if emergencies arise.

Since it is much more likely that you will be part of an emergency involving people living around you than yourself, let's assume that the emergency you have to deal with concerns a friend of yours, not you.

One emergency situation that occurs on college campuses with some frequency is alcohol poisoning. Someone goes to a party, drinks far more than they can handle, and collapses. It is essential that you call 911 immediately. I have heard of students hesitating to call 911 because they feared that the police would ticket them or their friend for being a minor in possession of alcohol. In the meantime, the friend lost precious minutes of urgently needed medical attention. If you find yourself in this situation, call 911 and get help immediately!

Another type of emergency situation involves a sexual assault. Your friend will need to get help if he or she has been sexually assaulted.

Medical, counseling, and criminal issues may be involved that need to be addressed. Most campuses have phone hotlines and special personnel with expertise in counseling victims of sexual assaults. In addition, most campus and city police today have officers who are specially trained to respond sensitively and thoroughly with individuals who are victims of sexual assault. The same is true at most hospital emergency rooms.

You may find yourself faced with a student you know who has a medical or psychiatric emergency. If you come upon a student who has collapsed, is having difficulty breathing, or is wounded and bleeding, immediately call 911 for emergency medical attention.

These kinds of emergency situations can often have some impact on a student's academic progress, even if it is short term. Encourage the student to contact his or her academic advisor or dean, or do so yourself. These administrators will alert the faculty that there is a legitimate reason why this student is not in class or will be turning in exams or assignments late. When the immediate emergency has passed, the student can then follow up with each individual faculty member to make whatever additional arrangements might be necessary.

For you, dealing with an emergency may be frightening, especially if it's the first time you've had to do so. You should feel confident, however, that college officials, medical and counseling staffs, and police officers are all well prepared for such situations and are there to help you out. They have considerable experience with these situations and will guide you and your friend on how to deal with the immediate emergency and any necessary follow-up.

80 Visit the Counseling and Health Centers

Your college has invaluable resources available to you to support your well-being so that you can focus on your academic studies. You should take full advantage of these resources and services because they will serve you well. Since your tuition and fees pay for these services, you shouldn't hesitate for even a second.

There are many reasons for visiting the counseling or health centers. The most obvious reason would be if you're ill or injured—if you have a fever, a sore throat, a broken arm, or a stomach flu. Go to the health center to see a doctor or nurse. They'll check your vital signs, examine you, and prescribe medications if needed.

You might also want to visit the health center if you need birth control devices, think you might be pregnant, or want to be tested for sexually transmitted diseases. You may come to college with previously diagnosed problems and need continuing treatment of headaches, eating disorders, vision problems, or depression.

Some colleges have a counseling center that is separate from the health center, but they are often closely integrated. Counseling centers schedule regular appointments but also almost always have walk-in hours when you can just drop in without an appointment and someone will be available to see you. Just like the health center, there is usually no cost or just a minimal payment to see a counselor. Several decades ago there was a stigma attached to seeing a counselor or therapist, but today quite the opposite is true.

Students go to the counseling center for a variety of reasons. You might be very homesick or might have a close relative at home who is not well and want to talk to someone about the situation. In the first weeks you might find that you are having trouble adjusting to being on your own and going to college, or your parents might call to tell you that they are filing for a divorce or that there are financial difficulties because one parent has been laid off from work. You might find yourself in a relationship for the first time and need someone to talk to about it, you might be in a relationship that is breaking up badly, or you might be in a relationship with a person who is manipulative and abusive.

Other students go to counseling or the health center to get help with eating disorders. If a student is sexually assaulted while on campus, the counseling center and health center are there to help. Some students are abusing drugs or are alcoholic, and when they are ready to seek help they may get coordinated support from both the counseling center and health center. Still other students are suicidal, and the counseling center can help them address those issues.

Sometimes, when students have academic problems, the cause may lie with issues that are not related to the classroom but need to be addressed in the counseling center. Some students have problems managing their money for the first time, and they need to talk with someone about how to get those issues, like credit card abuse, under better control.

These services are part of your college's resources. They are for you, not just for others. You pay for them, and you should take full advantage of them. If you're in doubt about whether your problem is serious enough to go to the health or counseling center, by all means err on the side of going for help. Getting routine help and support for your physical and emotional/mental health is part of growing up and becoming an adult. You're smart—use these services!

Family, Finances, and the Details of Daily Life

81 Write Home: Ask for Care Packages

You're enjoying your independence. You may miss home, but you want to show that you can be on your own. What are the rules about calling your parent(s)? Are you supposed to? Do you have to? If you do call, how often?

Meanwhile, you're busy. You've got a million things to do. You're excited about the first days and weeks of college. There's so much going on that you don't want to miss anything. Where do the parent(s) fit in all of this?

If you are living on campus, you should make a point of staying there, especially in the first weeks of college. Some students who live relatively close to campus travel home every weekend. That choice will rob you of the opportunity to fully invest emotionally in campus life, activities, and new friends. If you are at home most weekends, then college doesn't really become home; you don't achieve the valuable growth and separation from your home and high school experience.

It's important to stay in touch with your family because they will be a part of your life forever. Your parent(s) want to hear from you. They want to know if you're eating, staying healthy, and going to class. They are thinking about you, anxious about how you're adjusting, how you're finding the demands of college, and whether you're making friends. Even if there are issues you want to actively distance yourself from and people that you choose not to be close to, it would be an extreme case to choose to have no contact at all.

You need to decide how frequent and deep your contacts are, because every student will have a different kind of relationship with their parents. Students I know have many different ties with parent(s) in college. A small number of students call home to talk every day, even multiple times each day. Other students send e-mails or talk every few days or once a week. A very small number get in touch every month or every couple of months.

You have control over what you want to talk about with your family. You can ask for advice about classes, about relationships, about campus activities, and about finances. Or you might decide that all you want to share with your parent(s) is that you're alive and well and doing okay. That's much, much better than having no contact.

For their part, your parent(s) may have their own problems dealing with your leaving the house. It creates significant changes for them, and they will go through an adjustment period just like you. If you're the first to go to college, it signals a period of change in their lives, that their kids are growing up, as are they. If you're the sole child in the family or the last to go to college, then your parent(s) are in for an even greater adjustment, having to renew their adult lives and their married life as a twosome, if indeed they are married, or as a single individual living alone.

So, get in touch with your parent(s). While you're at it, ask them to send along a little care package. It's great to receive packages at college, whether they're large or small. Tell your parent(s) I said so. It'll give you a lift just when you need it, and it will make your parent(s) feel like they're needed and are still helping to raise you.

82 Make Your First Visit Home a Good Experience

When you go back home for the first time from college, you want it to be a good visit. Do your part to make sure it's as good as possible.

There will be a lot of excitement on everyone's part when you go home. You will be very engrossed in all the new things you are experiencing in college and will expect everyone to pay attention to you and your new life. Because there is so much new for you—whether you've been gone a week, a month, or a semester—you will want your family and friends to listen to your every word.

Yet at home, your siblings, friends, and perhaps even your parent(s) will want you to pay attention to their experiences as well. They will feel that they too have grown, changed, and developed new interests, and they will want you to be interested. However, you are likely to feel that no one has had as many new experiences or changed as much as you have. To you, things at home might look pretty much just like you left them. In many ways, you will be right, but still you will need to be ready to listen as well as share.

You should be ready for a fair amount of adjusting on your part and everyone else's. At college you are in charge of your life, and no one is ever checking on you or questioning what you are doing with your time or your personal space. At home, however, your parent(s) are the boss, or at least they think that they are. They will expect you to eat when they eat, clean up after yourself, help out around the house, and perhaps even be home at a certain hour.

You may also find that your family is ready for you to immediately settle back into familiar family patterns. That can be very comforting and reassuring, but at the same time, you may realize that you've moved beyond your old familiar patterns. Before you left home, all the advice you had received was to go out, become adult and independent, and explore the world around you at college. Why, now, when you return home, does it seem that there is so much pressure to conform to the old family ways?

The biggest jolt and most awkward moment may come when you tell your family that you have to begin making plans to return "home" by a certain day and time. While everyone, including you, may have been able to avoid facing the reality of your new life and independence, when you begin referring to your new college as "home," reality will hit.

The truth is that you don't have to choose so fast between your college home and your family home. Enjoy them both. There will certainly be some discomfort in these awkward moments, but you should take advantage of what is so special during this transition time. You still have the love of family and friends in the ways you have always enjoyed, and at the same time that love and friendship are growing and transforming from childhood/teenage relationships to adult relationships.

So, when you do go to see your parent(s), take full advantage and pleasure in what you remember most fondly. Whether it's good talks, a good bed, good friends, or good memories, enjoy them still. But be your new self, too, the person who is a bit older, wiser, and more experienced and who is learning to be independent.

If you can effectively manage the awkward moments and negotiate some minor conflicts, you can have two homes in college, one at your family's house and one at the college campus. Make both homes your favorite places to be.

83 Keep Your High School Friends but Invest in New College Friendships

High school was hopefully a wonderful experience for you, and you have some great memories from that time of your life. Now, however, it's time to move on with the rest of your life. Still, you want to be able to hold onto the good relationships you had with your closest friends and also maintain ties with other friends and acquaintances.

Your first priority must be to establish your independence and build new friendships in college. To do this and to keep good relationships with your best high school friends, it's best to room blind. Don't choose to room with someone you know from high school. It will inhibit your freedom to expand your horizons in college, and it may ruin a good friendship.

If there's just one other student or even a handful from your high school who are attending the same college as you, it's perfectly reasonable for you to want to live in the same residence hall as people you know. However, if you know ten or twenty or fifty students from your high school who are attending the same college as you, then you need to actively and intentionally stake out your independence.

I have known far too many students who relive their high school social and academic worlds in college because they never make the transition to college. They choose to live with friends from the same high school, choose classes with high school friends, and participate in social activities with the same people. All of these choices may provide you with security, but in fact you will be diminishing your chances to explore, grow, learn, and find your adult identity during your college years. While you may think that your parents have trouble letting go and treating you like an adult, one's peers often have the greatest difficulty doing so. You'll find yourself stuck in high school all over again.

It's great fun to run into high school friends at college or to meet at a party or football game. It's a wonderful reunion. The same is true when you go home for the first time in the fall, whether it's for a weekend, your fall break, or Thanksgiving. Enjoy your friends, share with them how you've grown, and tell them about all the new people, interesting classes, and exciting experiences you've had. Those friendships will grow and strengthen as long as you have the opportunity to grow and develop in college as an independent adult.

Seize your independence from your high school friends. Don't let the opportunity to grow socially as well as intellectually pass you by.

DEANNA NEWMAN—*"Should I Visit My Family
before Thanksgiving Vacation?"*

Deanna Newman prides herself on her independence. She loves her family but was very clear that she wanted to go away to college. She wanted to experience new things, new people, new surroundings, and especially some distance from her family.

When Deanna's parents dropped her off at the residence hall at college, she kissed them good-bye and firmly told them that she would be the one to initiate phone calls and e-mail messages. Her parents were great, but her mom had a tendency to be overinvolved, and her dad had always had too many rules and instructions when she lived at home. Deanna wanted to be on her own, without her mother knowing all the details of her life and without her father telling her what classes to take and when to be at home at night.

The first few days at college, before classes began, were somewhat lonely for Deanna. Sure, everyone was very friendly and nice, and there were lots of social activities, but there was also lots of dead space when she had nothing to do. It was ironic, but Deanna kind of missed her mother's questions about whom she was hanging out with and what her plans were. But Deanna held tough and didn't call home. Instead, she acted the part of the happy, carefree college student. Deanna went to the bookstore and bought her course books, opened a new bank account, and began to find her way around campus with some of the students from her hall.

After a week at college, Deanna called home. Her parents were so excited to hear from her, and Deanna, too, was delighted to talk with them. They talked for a long time, and everything seemed great. But then her mom started to ask what seemed to Deanna like too many personal questions, and her dad started up with his list of rules. Deanna ended the conversation somewhat abruptly. She felt great about being in touch with her parents but also a little bitter that they seemed just like from before she'd left home. Deanna was changing, and she had been on her own for a full week. Weren't her parents going to change, too?

The first weeks of college went reasonably well, but Deanna missed home a lot. She was surprised that she would miss her parents. She called home every week, and her conversations with her parents were both comforting and annoying. Deanna's parents told her they were really trying to respect her independence, but they certainly missed her and found it difficult not to talk more often. Deanna *was torn—on the one hand she missed her parents enormously, but on the other hand, she had promised herself that it was best to be independent.*

Deanna's next-door neighbor took the exact opposite approach. Jaime went home to visit her parents almost every weekend. She seemed to be really happy about her choice, but not being on campus on the weekends really left her out of the college social loop. Deanna wondered if maybe there was some middle ground that she should explore.

She decided on a compromise. There really was no reason that she couldn't talk to her parents more than once a week. "Maybe I'm being too rigid," she thought to herself. "Why can't I call home when I feel like I want to talk with them?" So Deanna decided to wait till Thanksgiving to go home to see her parents but called home and e-mailed whenever she felt like it. Her parents, after a time, also got permission to call and e-mail when they needed or wanted to, and everyone began to adjust their relationships so that they were more adult and reflected a transition from their parent-teenager home of the past few years.

Even though it hadn't been the easiest first months at college, Deanna was very pleased with herself. She was learning to live independently including taking responsibility for both the good and bad that went along with that. Deanna was growing up, becoming independent, and she was really excited to be at college.

84 Make Friends with Staff in the Financial Aid Office

A college education, whether it's public or private, is going to cost you and your family an enormous amount of money. For most of you, it's money you don't have. Hopefully, you've already made the correct and necessary decision that you should not forgo a college education because of the high price tag. However, to find a way to pay for college—whether through grants, loans, work-study, or a combination of all three—you will eventually end up dealing with your college financial aid office.

Welcome to the world of bureaucracy! Beginning with the infamous FAFSA form, you will be working with layers of organizations that provide financial aid funds. Your main contact will be your financial aid office, but along the way you will learn that the U.S. government and its various agencies, banks and loan institutions, sometimes state government, and various other offices are all part of the picture.

You and/or your parent(s) will need to be very organized about financial aid. It's a bad joke, but you almost need a college or even advanced degree to fill out these forms. Is the FAFSA form more complicated than doing your taxes? Probably. It certainly is when you face all those questions for the very first time. Get all your tax documents together way ahead of time and buy some file folders to keep all the records and correspondence that will take place in the years ahead.

You need to make a point of getting to know a counselor at the financial aid office. Make these people your friends, not your enemies. Their difficult task is to make sense of the myriad rules and regulations—and they change every year—and to try to assign the proper amount of aid to each applicant. They want to award you aid if you qualify. Treat them as people, not bureaucrats, and you will have much greater success and much less frustration in your efforts.

If ever there was a time and a place to ask questions, the financial aid process and office is it. When you first start working on the FAFSA form, come to the office with your questions. When you get financial aid notification letters that are at all unclear, call the office and ask them to explain—I've seen some that were written in a language that isn't taught in any English class I've ever known.

Importantly, if you disagree with the financial aid office's assessment of your earnings or if you are concerned that the award you have received isn't sufficient, call the office. You'll probably be frustrated or discouraged (especially if you're put on hold), but don't shout at them. In almost all cases, they will be happy to review your file with you and offer various alternatives for you to think about in terms of financial aid.

During the academic year or when tuition bills arrive, if the award doesn't show up or if you haven't received the amount you expected, don't panic. Just walk over to the financial aid office to look at your file. Bring all your well-organized financial aid files with you to help make your case. In the event you need an emergency loan or if you've overspent part of your budget that should have gone toward financial aid, talk with someone in this office for advice on how to proceed.

Colleges want you to have enough funds to pay tuition. Think of them as your allies in the financial aid game. Most likely you won't get as much aid as you want or need, but the financial aid counselors want to be sure you are treated as fairly as the regulations will allow. They also want you to graduate college and have a rewarding experience. This is a very important relationship for you. Make it a good one.

85 Be Careful Using Credit Cards

Credit cards are not free money. They are not birthday gifts from a bank. They represent *your* money, and every dollar *you* spend, *you* will have to repay, often with high interest.

Credit cards are a way of life today and, when used properly, are perfectly fine. They can provide an excellent alternative to carrying cash or checks with you.

The problem is that college students are notorious for misusing credit cards. Nevertheless, when you arrive on campus you will see all kinds of come-ons inviting you to sign up for any number of credit cards, even offering you a free gift to do so.

The challenge facing you is to manage your credit carefully and not to abuse it. First, you should ask the bank to set a low credit limit to help you from overspending. Second, you should only spend money on credit that you have set aside in your budget to spend. While banks may encourage you to overspend by offering low initial terms on interest rates, you need to know that that is how banks make money from credit cards. Those interest rate payments are what ruin people. You gain the advantage over the banks if you spend only an amount that you can pay off in full with every monthly bill.

If this is the first time you've had a credit card, you may be overwhelmed by the opportunity to go online or into a store, see something you want to buy, and buy it without paying cash, just credit. That's the trap that far too many college students (and adults as well) fall into—be sure to avoid it. If you don't have the money to pay for an item in a store, don't buy it. The second trap is that you are likely to forget today what you purchased on your credit last week or even yesterday, and as a result, your monthly bill will shock you out of your mind. You won't be able to afford to pay much beyond the minimum payment due, and you'll be stuck in the world of owing high interest rate payments in addition to your monthly charges. Be ever so careful.

If you find you don't have control over your spending habits, go see a college counselor and talk to the bank that issues the credit card. Get rid of your credit card—cut it up into pieces and throw it away until you can get a better handle on your spending. You should also review what went wrong so that in the future you learn to take more control over your spending and finances. In the meantime, work out a realistic plan to pay off the credit card bill. Do not dip into your tuition payments or financial aid to pay for credit card purchases. Don't ruin your careful plans to pay for college by needlessly buying new clothes and electronics on credit with money you don't have.

Be sensible about credit cards. Use them wisely, as if they were cash in your pocket. If you even think you might have a problem paying off your monthly bill, get help immediately from parents, counselors, and the bank. And, finally, keep track of your bill and send in your payment promptly so you are credited with an on-time payment.

86 Balance Your Checkbook

It seems simple enough. You have put money in the bank and opened a checking account in your own name. You write checks, you keep track of the checks you've written in your check ledger, and you balance your bank statement when it comes in the mail each month. But sometimes what seems simple in theory isn't so simple in practice.

You have to write so many checks in the first few days of college. You write checks to the bookstore, to the residence hall for computing services, to the student government, and to stores to buy printer cartridges, notebooks, pens, posters, and other things for your room that you didn't bring from home. Organizations are selling T-shirts that you feel you just have to own and wear to demonstrate school spirit.

You're also very busy all the time. You have orientation meetings to attend, welcome week activities, floor meetings, and athletic events—all before classes have even begun. You stay up late at night going to parties and talking with people you hope will become your friends. Your adrenalin is running high, and you're anxious about classes and meeting new people.

Oh, and then there's that business of balancing your checkbook. It's not surprising that this task falls to the bottom of your to-do list. It's not interesting, challenging, or fun. It's definitely not a priority in the midst of all the exciting, new events that are happening all around you.

However, if you don't watch your checking balance, then you're likely to spend more than you have in the bank. The bank then will not honor your checks, and they will bounce. The bank will charge you high fees for bouncing checks, your credit will sink with the local businesses, and you'll be wasting a lot of unnecessary time on money matters instead of academic and social matters.

Here's what you should do. Every time you write a check, write down the check number and date, the recipient, and the amount. As soon as you get back to your room in the residence hall, write down all that information in your check ledger and subtract the amount of the new checks from your previous balance. Now you know how much you have left in your checking account.

It's hard to make good estimates for regular spending in the first days and weeks of college. After a few weeks, however, you should have a pretty good idea of what you want, what you need, and what you can afford to spend. Make a daily, weekly, or monthly budget for yourself and try to hold to it.

If you are attentive to balancing your checkbook, then you can go forward confidently each day knowing your financial status. It won't make you any richer, but it will save you from making costly spending mistakes, allow you to plan your finances, and give you confidence about your ability to manage your money.

87 Get a Job

There are many good reasons to work during your college years. Working to earn money to pay for college is only the most obvious.

Be careful not to work more than about twenty hours a week if you are attending college full time to avoid negatively affecting your academic performance. Ten to twelve hours per week is probably a more manageable load if you can get by financially.

Work in college can take many forms, and you can learn from each job you have. Work gives structure to your life, and by working in college, you become grounded in the ways of the world yet remain largely protected from society's realities.

Work gives you a regular schedule, regular responsibilities, and clear accountability in terms of being paid hourly for doing a good hour's work. It will typically put you in regular contact with people outside your age group, which is a healthy contrast to the traditional college environment, where most of your time is spent with people who are of a very narrow age bracket.

Work also gives you a chance to be in contact with people from different social and economic backgrounds. If you work on the facilities or dining hall staff, you'll be with people who come from a range of economic backgrounds, some like your own and others from higher or lower economic classes. If you work in the hospital or a mall, you will also encounter professionals and clients who represent cross-sections of the population.

Working during college—at the same time that you're trying to figure out your identity issues, concentration/major, and career plans—allows you to try out different types of jobs. How does it feel to work in the service or retail sector, in the science lab, in the library, or as a teacher's assistant? What do you observe when you work in a doctor's clinic in a hospital, a law firm, a nonprofit organization, or for a professor doing research? These experiences will give you constructive insight, sometimes affirming and other times challenging your professional goals.

If you do not need to work for tuition, you may want to be slightly more selective about your hours and the kind of work you do. You may choose to wait to work till summer vacation or until your second year of college. You might decide to pursue an interesting internship for which you will be paid little or even nothing for your work. The luxury of not having to work doesn't mean that you should miss out on the opportunity to do so.

That's right. Think of work during college as an opportunity, not as a burden. You will learn a great deal from the experience if you take the time to reflect on it in light of your classes and personal development and values. It will prepare you for future positions and will look very good on your résumé. Approach work positively. Not only will you learn and grow, but you will also be earning money to pay for college costs and, in some cases, for a little spending money.

88 Pick Up after Yourself: Do Your Own Laundry

When you move into your room in the residence hall and throw some socks on the floor, guess what? They will not move until you pick them up. When you've gone through all your shirts and underwear and your laundry bag is full, it will be up to you to find a washing machine to clean them. Want to wear an ironed blouse? Then you'll be the one ironing.

Have you ever wondered how your family's house stayed clean, how your clothes got washed and ironed before they reappeared in your closet, or how your floor got vacuumed? Hopefully, you know the answer because you were taking responsibility for cleaning up after yourself at home. If that's not the case, though, you're in for a big shock.

Learning to clean up after yourself is a valuable lesson to pick up in college if you haven't already had to learn it at home. Even if you can afford to pay a vendor to do your laundry and ironing in college, you should resist the temptation. If you live close enough to home to take your laundry home to your mother or father, don't do it except in an emergency. These are good life lessons: it is important to know how to take care of your basic needs.

Now that you are not living in your family's home, you are the king or queen of your room, and you make the rules. If you don't clean up, only you have to live with the consequences; if you wear dirty or smelly clothes, you'll be the one smelling the roses.

Of course, you may find there's more than a little peer pressure to stay on the clean and neat side of things. Your roommates, for instance, may have very different standards than you. They may strongly object to your clothes being strewn across the floor or hanging over the couch and desk chairs. Don't be surprised if they find it gross when you don't throw out your moldy cheese in the refrigerator or you leave your cereal bowl, silverware, and glasses in the sink unwashed. At the same time, they might also object if you're the opposite extreme and you vacuum and dust each day and complain when they don't fold their clothes neatly or make their beds.

Your personal habits quickly become everyone's business on the floors and suites of the residence hall. Your peers will know more about your personal habits than you ever wished, and they'll talk about them. Peer pressure can be far more powerful than your father or mother asking you to clean up your room.

Most important, however, is that you realize that you are responsible for taking care of yourself. As an adult, the responsibility for how you look, how your clothes appear, and how clean or dirty you keep your room is all yours. Your choices in these matters reflect on you and give people instant impressions about how you think about yourself. They will affect your relationships with roommates and friends and your own self-esteem and self-worth. It's part of becoming an adult.

TONY MANCUSO — *"Why Do They Charge So Much Interest?"*

Tony Mancuso comes from a solid middle-class family. His dad is a high school teacher, and his mom works part-time as a secretary. They live in a good neighborhood and are very proud to own their home. Tony had never needed for anything, though he never asked for too much, either.

Tony received a good financial aid package from his college, and he had already arranged to work ten to twelve hours per week to earn all his work-study funds. His parents had put away money each year for many years in order to afford to send Tony to college. The last few years they had passed up special vacations, let house repairs go undone, and essentially held off on buying things for themselves in order to save for Tony.

Tony had talked with his dad about finances for college, and together they had come up with a good budget to get him through. There would be money for tuition, room and board in the residence hall, and books for his classes. Tony was responsible for contributing a portion of the funds for tuition each year from his summer employment, and any spending money was to come from his work-study position.

When Tony arrived at college, he was amazed at how wealthy many of his peers seemed to be. It wasn't just that they didn't need to work but that they were dressed in the latest fashions and their rooms in the residence hall looked like an upscale electronics showroom. If they didn't like the food in the cafeteria, it was nothing for them to head off to one of the fancy downtown restaurants. Tony wasn't so much jealous as in shock.

Tony went down to the college bookstore to buy course books and school supplies. Lined up parallel to the long row of students waiting to get into the bookstore were student representatives from various credit card companies sitting at tables offering all kinds of great stuff just for applying for a credit card—free phone cards, free T-shirts, discounts on airfare.

Tony had never had a credit card and he didn't think he would qualify for one. So he was surprised when the representative told him that college students are good credit risks, so he would likely be approved. The same student representative explained to him that it was important for him to establish credit at a young age.

Tony knew that his father would be proud of him for taking advantage of this seemingly great opportunity. He applied for three credit cards, got all the gifts they were offering, and waited to hear. Within ten days, Tony received letters from each of the credit card companies saying he had been approved and containing a credit card.

Tony started to use his credit cards right away. After all, you only build credit by spending money is how he understood the credit business. At first he was somewhat cautious, buying only things that he already had money to pay for. For instance, he bought his course books with the credit card because his father had sent him money for books. Soon, however, he realized that he could use the credit card to buy things in advance of his getting paid at his work-study job because the credit card company wouldn't bill till the end of the month.

Tony started to buy new clothes, new running shoes, pizza, dinner out—all kinds of things. It was so great. He could behave and hang out just like the wealthier kids around him without their having to know his financial situation. He could just flash his credit card, and the bill was paid. This was fun!

Then the bills started coming. This was not fun! In fact, it was kind of daunting. Tony sat on his bed in disbelief at how much the credit card companies said he owed. "How could I owe that much money?" he thought. "There's no way I spent all that much." He went over the charges again and again, until he was completely persuaded that he had indeed spent all that money.

Fortunately, Tony figured out that he only had to pay the minimum charge each month. Not only did he not have the money to pay the full amount of the bills, but there was no way he was going to tell his parents about this. So he paid the minimum amount due on each bill and felt like he had this all figured out. He even decided to use only one of his credit cards and put the others in his drawer.

Then, next month the bills came again. Tony was shocked. He had never realized that there would be such a steep interest charge on the amount he owed. Tony knew that interest would be charged, but now he saw what that meant in terms of dollars and cents. He was thousands of dollars in debt—and this wasn't for tuition or room and board. He didn't know how he could ever pay it off. He was further behind this month than last. Tony broke into a heavy sweat.

Tony decided he had to phone his father. It wasn't an easy call. They had a *very long talk. After his father cooled off a bit, he told Tony to see his financial aid officer. That person set him up with a counselor who helped Tony understand what had happened and how to prevent such an occurrence in the future. The counselor also helped Tony refocus his attention on his studies, which he had largely forgotten about in the midst of all his financial worries.*

In time, Tony got back his father's confidence and respect. After a couple of years, he also had paid off his credit card bills in full. Tony's grades picked up, as did his self-esteem. Tony had gotten a big shock coming to college, one he hadn't expected. Still, he recovered from it, learned some good lessons, went on to a very successful college career and eventually a good credit rating.

89 Show Up to Class

Yes, it's important to go to class in college. In fact, you should plan to attend every scheduled class session. It is your choice to attend college, and it is the opportunity of a lifetime. You should take advantage of every chance you have to learn.

As a person who is attending college, you obviously were a good student in high school and rarely missed classes. However, if you did purposefully miss class in high school, besides legitimate reasons like sickness or holidays, you probably felt that skipping class was a sign of rebellion or independence. School was a requirement; it was something you had to attend because someone else wanted you to, so by not going to class you were harming someone else, not yourself.

You need to think about college quite differently. To be worthwhile, college has to be *your* choice. If you don't want to be in college, then by all means save yourself and your parent(s) a lot of money and time and take a leave of absence. However, as long as you are in college, you should remember that each course you take holds immense possibilities, and you should want to be there for each session.

Most of my students do attend class every session. But I have had some students tell me that they will have to miss class because they have to rush their sorority, or they are in the midst of organizing a campus event, or are having difficulty waking up in time for a ten o'clock class. These students are attempting to be polite and respectful by telling me about their absences in advance. However, I am always struck by these excuses because it tells me that these students have badly misplaced their priorities for college.

Rushing a sorority may be important to you, but as a priority it should come after your academic work. It's very important to be involved in extracurricular activities, but you have to keep in mind which college activities are central and which are *extra*. Staying up late at night is a college rite of passage for many, but it's no substitute for being able to get up in the morning to go to class. You can't learn from class if you don't attend because you've overslept.

Embrace the opportunity you have to attend college. Be sure to take advantage of every opportunity available to you. But keep your eye on the academic prize, even while you get involved in the whole of the college learning experience. The first step is to attend classes.

90 Use a Planner

You will need to keep track of a tremendous number of things going on in your life during college. The only one who will be worrying that you show up where you are supposed to be and when you're supposed to be there will be you.

A planner is one good way to help you keep track of your life. Electronic or paper planners allow you to keep a record of all of your classes, work hours, extracurricular activities, organizational meetings, study groups, exercise, and sports. You can enter due dates for papers, exams, and various class assignments. You can block out time for social events (parties, football games, coffee with friends) and time just to be alone. Be sure to leave time to eat and sleep.

Although many middle and high schools in recent years have encouraged students to regularly use planners, many students still resist. Sometimes the resistance comes from feeling too busy to take time to write down appointments and schedules. That's a sure sign that you need one.

Another reason some people don't use planners is because they don't believe their schedule is so complicated that they need a reminder to keep track of their lives. They don't understand that college is very different from high school in terms of people's routines. In high school you woke up, went to school, maybe had one or more activities after class, and then went home to do homework for the next day.

In college, your classes will start at a different time every day, and there will be breaks during the day when you will need to study, go to faculty office hours, or meet with friends. You may have night classes, study groups, or a work schedule to remember. Your bedtime may vary tremendously, and there will be numerous evening activities to keep in mind.

The other big difference is that you are on your own. There is no parent to wake you in the morning or remind you about a big sporting event coming up. No one will be checking to see that you get to class on time or attend a meeting where people are counting on you to be there.

You will have to take much more responsibility for your schedule, and your schedule will be much fuller and more varied. Let a planner give you a little support to manage your life. After all, *you* are the one who is scheduling your exciting and very full life, so you don't want to miss out on all that you have planned.

91 Love Your Laptop

You need to be computer literate when you come to college. If you aren't using a computer at the time you read this book, go out and get emergency instruction either before you enter college or in the first days of orientation and welcome week.

What kind of computer should you use? By the time you finish reading this tip, the best advice on which computer to use will have changed three times. If you are computer literate you will be able to quickly adapt to any new computer system or software.

Should you purchase a computer or use computers available for public use on campus? If you can afford a computer, go out and buy one to bring to college. Do know that its shelf life won't last much past your college education. If you can't afford to purchase a computer, don't worry, because almost all colleges are well equipped with public computer sites for college students.

The most important thing about computers is that you need to be completely comfortable with yours. You will spend more hours than you can imagine in front of your computer screen. Learn to take full advantage of all the power and systems on your computer. You will use your computer for every class you take, and you will turn to it for social activities and entertainment. It will be your main source of contact and communication with parent(s), friends from home, and even friends on campus.

A laptop is particularly valuable because of its versatility. You will find yourself bringing it to class to take notes. You will bring it to organizational meetings to keep track of committee business. You will carry it in your backpack and have it with you when you go to the library to study. You will use it when you meet friends for study groups or to collaborate on a paper.

The one disadvantage to laptops is that they are easily stolen. Be sure to lock it to your desk in your room in the residence hall when you go out. When you have it in your backpack, never lose sight of it. The college library is a high-theft area, so never leave your computer unattended on a study table or cubicle when you run to find a book or go to the bathroom.

You'll be a far happier student if you learn to embrace your computer rather than resist its full usage. You and your computer will spend many hours of every day and night together throughout your years in college. Take good care of this loyal companion.

Looking beyond
the First Year

92   Identify Faculty Who Will Write
Recommendation Letters for You

Every job, internship, and graduate school will ask you to provide references. After you're in college, it will no longer be good enough to get a letter from your favorite high school teacher, the manager of the store in your local shopping mall where you worked, your clergyperson, or a friend of the family who has seen you grow up and flourish.

Faculty members (and graduate student instructors) at your college will be the most important source of recommendation letters for you during your college years and beyond. You will find that you need these letters as early as your first and second years of college. If you are looking for a summer internship, a research assistantship, acceptance to a study abroad program, or a job in the library, you will be asked to provide a letter from a faculty member on your campus.

Later, when you apply to graduate school or a professional school program, it is critical that you can turn to at least two or three faculty members who will write outstanding letters on your behalf.

Most faculty will be more than willing to write one or even multiple letters for you, but only if you have developed a relationship with them or have caught their attention through your comments in class discussion, by writing an exceptional paper, or by visiting office hours.

A small number of very special faculty, usually those who have been so impressed with you that they are willing to serve as your champions, will go out of their way and initiate calls and contacts on your behalf. They will keep you in mind when they hear of scholarship opportunities, summer internships, special study programs, and research assistantships. They will make it their business to be sure you get into the best graduate programs.

Some faculty will be willing to write letters but will not be reliable about deadlines. You need to keep tabs on whether the letters you have requested have been submitted in a timely manner. If you can't depend on a faculty member to write a letter for you on time, then you are better off finding a replacement.

When you do ask for a letter, you want to make the process as easy as possible for the faculty member. If you like this professor so much that you are asking for a reference letter, it's likely that many other students are as well, and your letter is just one of several that the professor is writing. Tell your professor what jobs, programs, or graduate schools you are applying to and give him or her a copy of your résumé, any forms that need to be filled out (usually you will have to complete part of the forms), a short written reminder about the purpose of the letter, and the due date. If it's possible to send the letter via e-mail or through a Web site, ask your professor if he or she would prefer to send a letter this way or by snail mail. If the latter, include a stamped, addressed envelope for the professor to use. Let your professor know the eventual outcome of your applications—he or she will be interested to hear.

The key to asking for reference letters is to know faculty well enough that you can approach them. Your first task in securing references as a first-year student is building your relationships with faculty. After you've done that, don't be shy about asking for letters. Faculty will be pleased and honored that you have asked and will be eager to learn that you have succeeded in your job search or pursuit of advanced graduate and professional degrees.

93 Explore Possible Majors

Sometime during the sophomore year, most colleges will ask you to declare your major or concentration. Some students come into college very certain about what they want to study. Most, however, come to college wanting to explore a wide range of subject areas and topics and are undecided about a major.

Students who have already decided their field of study prior to coming to college may have applied and enrolled in schools such as art, engineering, or nursing. Even within those schools, however, students will need to make decisions about subfields of study during their undergraduate years.

Another group of students who often appear certain about their choice of major are those who are considered preprofessional. Students who plan to attend law school often major in political science, and those interested in a career in business often choose economics. These students limit their choice of majors as a result of the widespread myth that it's essential to have those particular majors in order to gain admission to law or business school, respectively. That is simply not the case. Choose a major in a field that you find stimulating, not one that holds little or no interest for you.

Students planning to apply to medical school are required to complete many prerequisites during their undergraduate studies. Unlike their preprofessional peers in law and business, many of these highly competitive students feel pressured to double- or triple-major in order to look good on their medical school applications, so they choose to major in a science discipline like biology as well as a discipline in the social sciences or humanities. It's not necessary for you to double-major, but at least for these more narrowly focused students, it allows them to get a broader liberal arts education.

The largest group of students arrive at college undecided about their major. For most undergraduates, I think that's the preferred approach.

College is intended to be a time of exploration. Most high school curricula provide little opportunity to even begin to imagine the vast world of ideas and fields of study. Both preprofessional and undecided students are well known for changing their minds about their major multiple times during their college careers. Don't think of that as a problem. It's a natural step in the decision-making process as you take intriguing courses in new fields and then begin to pursue those subject areas in greater depth.

As a first-year student you should attempt to take courses in a wide variety of fields, and you should take those courses whose descriptions you find most interesting—or, even better, with professors who've been recommended to you as excellent teachers. You will also feel some pressure to complete general education or distribution requirements during your first couple of years. Rather than feeling overwhelmed, you should take a strategic approach, trying to fulfill your own mission of exploring broadly while also fulfilling your college's requirements. If your college has a good general education or distribution program, this should be a very easy task, because the general education requirements will overlap to a large extent with your own choices.

In your first year of college, keep your focus on exploration and breadth. Carry the idea of choosing a major in the back of your mind, but don't stress about it. It's a long way from your first semester till the time you decide on your major. Enjoy this stage of your college education, when you have the chance to take outstanding courses in the widest variety of fields.

94 Avoid the Sophomore Slump

It happens. The sophomore slump is for real. Your first year of college is an adrenaline rush, filled with new courses, new people, new activities, and a tremendous surge of independence.

Sophomore year comes along and most students expect the rush to carry them, just like the first year. The problem is that eventually the rush dissipates, your energy dwindles, and the forward thrust of your first year of college slows down, often dramatically. It's not that anything negative takes place, just that the surge of excitement of all the newness and independence begins to wear off.

The challenge of the sophomore year is to learn from all your new experiences and to begin to take control and responsibility as an adult for your independence and your choices, academic and otherwise. The rush of the first year of college must now be transformed into intrinsic motivation and commitment about your choices as an adult. The excitement and enthusiasm that reflected your adrenaline rush must now be sustained as part of your continuing approach to academics, social experiences, and the rich and full life that lies ahead of you.

The sophomore slump does happen to many students, it's not a myth. For some it will come earlier in the year and for some later. You may feel good about everything but just more sluggish. You may still like all the courses you're taking but find it's harder to do all the reading. You may be involved in great organizations but experience less of a thrill in taking on loads of responsibility.

I don't know if you can avoid the sophomore slump altogether, but you can certainly minimize the experience. The first step is for you to acknowledge the likelihood that you will experience a slump in your second year. The second step is to plan for some new challenges and experiences for your second year and to identify those continuing practices that were most meaningful to you in your first year.

What new challenges might you take on in your sophomore year? You could sign up for a new research experience or a study abroad project. You might decide to take on a leadership role in a campus organization to further develop your skills. You could look forward to a new living situation with friends or even to expanding your current group of friends. You might look forward to taking some new courses, either because you've completed the necessary prerequisites or because you now know which are the best professors and you want to study with them. Maybe what you need to do to minimize the slump is play a sport or pick up a musical instrument or plan for a great summer internship.

All of these choices take you a step beyond your first-year experiences, presenting you with new and stimulating personal, social, and intellectual challenges. They will make the sophomore year different from the first year of college, and you will feel confident that your life as a college student and adult will be new and interesting every year. You will have taken control and responsibility for your education and life path to an extent that you couldn't have imagined just a few years ago. This is no slump; you're living a great life.

CYNTHIA KINGSTON — *"What Should I Be When I Grow Up?"*

For a year now, everyone—her parents, her friends, her teachers—had been asking Cynthia Kingston where she intended to go to college. The attention was initially very nice, but then her neighbors, her aunt whom she hadn't talked to in three years, people in stores whom she didn't even know—everyone seemed to want to know where she was going to attend college. What a relief it was when she finally was able to answer this question!

But by the time summer rolled around, Cynthia started to hear a new question over and over again, and it just about freaked her out. People now wanted to know what she was going to do with her life after college! They wanted a quick answer about her career plans. "All of these questions about my career," Cynthia thought, "and I haven't even attended my first day of class yet!"

Cynthia knew what people wanted to hear. Her father was a well-known corporate attorney, a senior partner in a prestigious law firm. Everyone was hoping and even expecting, actually, that she would one day join her father's law firm.

Cynthia, in fact, had thought about her career during her life. At different times she had wanted to be a schoolteacher, health care worker, and tennis superstar. The problem was that she had thought about most of these career options when she was less than ten years old and, as far as tennis was concerned, it was clear she'd be spending more time in front of her TV watching the sport and eating snacks than receiving a paycheck for playing.

Oh, yes, she also had law in the back of her mind, too.

However, the last couple of years Cynthia had been focused on friends and college. She'd worried about taking the right courses, studying, getting good grades, enduring standardized tests, and, most recently, filling out college applications. Now that she had chosen a college, she had thought she would have a chance to rest, relax, and not think about any big questions. So the questions about a career came as one big, unexpected, and unwelcome surprise.

When Cynthia arrived at college, she found a mixed bag of ideas about careers. A good number of students could name their intended career areas—business, law, health care, education. Those were some of the big ones. A few even reported that they had known what careers they wanted since elementary school and, remarkably, still wanted to pursue that goal. But Cynthia soon learned that most students changed their minds quickly and frequently, even during the first semester of college.

Most of Cynthia's academic advisors and professors counseled against making a career choice too quickly. They pointed out that college is a time to take time, to think through one's professional and career goals as an adult, and to explore broadly one's likes and dislikes. They spoke of finding out about one's self, identity, skills, and interests—particularly those that could be sustained over time. This was comforting.

However, some preprofessional academic programs required students to get on track early in college. Some students were busy taking their premed, engineering, or prebusiness courses right away, in their first semester of college. But Cynthia understood that many other students who were interested in business, law, education, and so on planned to take a liberal arts curriculum and pursue those more focused, career pursuits later on, as juniors and seniors; through their majors; via internships; or in graduate school. The premed and engineering students, she learned, had less flexibility than others, but they also had a lot more opportunity to take a range of courses than they had believed when they first started college.

Cynthia took a deep breath. She knew she was a responsible person. She knew, too, that even though law was definitely an option and a great opportunity, she really didn't know what she wanted to do for her professional career. She decided to take her time to adjust to college and do well in her studies. There was so much exciting about college that she didn't want to miss. Great courses and faculty, midnight conversations, concerts, parties, new relationships, extracurriculars, study abroad, internships—she was looking forward to all of this.

Along the way, Cynthia was certain she would begin to find her direction, her goals, her passions, and her career. Cynthia knew where the career center was located and would find her way there when she was ready. She also knew where her father's law firm was located if she wanted to talk with anyone there. For now, she was going to think about her first semester of college and leave the rest of her life for a little later down the road.

95 Spend Your Summers Productively

In high school, summer meant time for vacation and work. Your parent(s) chose your vacation—to an amusement park, to a swimming pool, to visit relatives, to camp, or traveling cross-country. Your work was based on what was available in your hometown, perhaps selling clothes at the mall, waiting tables at the diner, being a lifeguard at a local pool, or doing office work for a family friend.

In college you will have much greater control of your summer choices, and the opportunities are plentiful. If possible, it's good to be strategic about your summers, because there are a very limited number of them during the college years.

Sometimes the best choice, if you've had a very intense academic year, is to take some time off to do nothing. Clear your head, get some sleep, rest your body and your brain. That's a reasonable plan, at least for a week or two. After that, you'll find yourself extremely bored with yourself and increasingly annoying to your family and friends.

Colleges offer all kinds of stimulating summer learning programs. There are study abroad opportunities and research assistantships with faculty on campus or abroad. Some college departments have special field classes, such as literature and creative writing programs at camp-like sites off campus or geological or oceanographic expeditions to interesting sites in the mountains or oceans.

Some students choose to stay on campus during all or part of the summer rather than return to their parents' homes. They may, of course, enroll in regular summer classes. Most students who stay on campus look for cheap housing but also want to make money to pay for summer expenses as well as for expenses during the coming year. There are jobs at local businesses but also opportunities to work on campus in research labs, in residence hall kitchens, in orientation programs, giving campus tours, in libraries, and doing groundskeeping work.

Many students return to their parents' homes during the summer. They may wish to be back at home with their families, but they also try to maximize their summer earnings by not paying for room and board. At home, they may continue to work at jobs they held during high school or to return as counselors to camps they had attended when younger. Other students, particularly in professional schools, get help finding well-paying summer work related to their engineering or business studies.

Internships in your projected professional field are another great use of your summer time. Your college may be able to help you find internships, but you should plan on doing the bulk of researching what's available and asking for and filling out applications on your own. Internships may be paid or volunteer—be sure to ask. You might work in the offices of a state or national governmental office, a nonprofit agency, a business, or an environmental organization.

It's important that you think ahead about your overall summer plans during college and plan ahead early each year to be sure you can actually find the job, internship, study abroad program, or whatever that you are seeking. It's good to take at least a short break from your studies and to get some physical distance from your college campus at some point during the summer. In addition to all the exciting summer opportunities that await you, you definitely want a chance to get refreshed and renewed before you return for the next year of academic studies.

96 Investigate Internships

One of the best opportunities you can pursue during your college years is an internship experience.

Internships provide you with invaluable work experience in a field of interest to you. They give you an insider's view of what it means to come to work every day in a professional organization and field that you may wish to pursue throughout your career. Even if you choose an internship that is not in your chosen field, it will give you firsthand insights about a field that you would otherwise know only through books, newspapers, and word of mouth.

It takes a lot of time and effort to secure a summer internship. Start early. Begin working on this early in the fall semester if you hope to have an internship the next summer. You first need to investigate what opportunities exist in fields that hold some interest for you. Then you need to learn more about what qualities are desirable in an intern. You will want to update your résumé and revise it numerous times to fit the specific needs of the various internships to which you are applying. Write a letter that explains both your interest in the internship and the qualifications and skills that you will bring to the position. You will need to send out many letters and make many calls to hope to be offered even one internship opportunity, but one is all you need.

Your academic department or campus career center also will likely assist you in identifying internship programs. They may have specific internship programs in governmental offices in your state or in Washington, D.C., or in industry, engineering, or nonprofit organizations. Take advantage of whatever programs or advice these offices have to offer you.

Internships may be paid, unpaid, or for college credit. Some organizations may have one paid internship position and several unpaid positions. If you need to earn money in the summer, then be sure to apply only to those that offer paid internships, and keep your options open to paying positions instead of an internship. Some government, foundation, and corporate programs pay a generous stipend for full-time summer internships at designated nonprofit service organizations, for research, or in corporate offices. A few internships will offer free or inexpensive housing for their interns, but others will require you to pay for your own housing in addition to volunteering your time. Most internships do expect you to volunteer your time in exchange for giving you the rich organizational experience you will receive.

In addition to all the education you will receive, if you do an outstanding job at your internship, your supervisor will serve as an excellent reference for you when it is time for you to go on the job market. Some interns impress their supervisors so much that they even get hired at that office when they graduate college.

Do consider spending one of your summers working in an internship. You will enjoy the overall experience and the people you work with, and you will learn invaluable lessons from both the positive and the negative aspects of the experience.

97 Graduate in Four Years or as Quickly Thereafter as Possible

College is one of life's great experiences. However, if you can manage it, limit this great experience to four years and move on to life's next great adventures. Doing so will also save you a bundle of money.

There are certainly many good reasons to stay in college beyond four years. One reason is financial need, which can force you to postpone your education because you cannot afford to pay for college expenses. A second reason is that you are working or supporting a family and cannot afford, financially or in terms of time, to attend school full time. A third good reason is that you or family members have health problems that require you to care for yourself or others. A fourth good reason is that you change your major and require additional time to complete your degree or preprofessional requirements. A fifth good reason is that you received an inadequate education in high school and consequently spent part of your first year in college taking remedial courses, slowing down your progress toward your degree.

Some students are delayed in their progress toward their degree because their college does not offer a sufficient number of courses in required fields each semester to allow all interested students to complete their degree requirements in a timely fashion. If that's your situation, you should complain to your institutional leaders—that's not acceptable.

You should make the most of your college education in a timely fashion. There is a rhythm and a community to a four-year college education. If you stay much beyond your fourth year, you will begin to lose your sense of a scholarly community and move toward a modality of course fulfillment and completing credits. Those are the necessary instrumental mechanisms of a college degree, but alone they do not represent a vibrant intellectual community.

Some students change their majors several times or are not certain about a professional path. That's fine; it's not a problem. However, if you are in this situation, you should try to complete your degree within five years. If your fifth year of college study brings greater clarity to your direction, then taking that extra year will have been a good choice.

Sometimes you will find that the key to the puzzle of discovering a compelling direction will be found more easily outside of college. If you haven't found your way early in college or still have no direction after a fifth year of college, you should begin exploring unfinished questions outside of the college arena. You may want to take a year off to travel, work at different types of jobs, or get on-the-job training with a corporate business. Within a year or two, you should have a better idea of what field interests you and what you want to pursue as you complete your college degree.

Set four years as your goal for completion of your degree, and focus your efforts on realizing all the benefits of college within that time frame. Be attentive to course requirements and consult regularly with your academic advisor. You may have good reason to extend your education beyond four years, and you shouldn't stress about doing so, but to the extent that you have control over matters, get the most out of these four years and be done. As wonderful as everyone hopes that college will be for you, there are great things ahead of you beyond college.

98 If Necessary, Look Into Transferring to Another College

You may find that you are one of those students who wants or needs to change schools after your first or second year of college. Any number of reasons might require you to consider transferring to a different college. Examine this possibility carefully, thoughtfully, and dispassionately so that you make the best decision, and be sure to keep your options open as you begin the process of applying to other schools.

You may find that you're not happy at the college you are attending or that you're reasonably happy but not fully satisfied with your educational and social experience. In either case, you want to carefully examine the reasons why that's the case. Changing colleges is a perfectly reasonable option, but you want to be certain it's the right choice for you.

You may find that the college you are attending is not the right fit for you. You should be sure that your feeling is persistent, that your unhappiness is not a reaction to one particular incident or event, such as a bad roommate situation, a low grade on a test, a professor's critical comments in class, being rejected for a part in a play, or not getting bids to join any fraternities. These circumstances and others like them can make you feel like you're not wanted at this college. However, you want to ascertain whether they are indicative of a campus culture that is not a good fit for you overall or whether you will be able to get past these unhappy moments to enjoy all that is good about the environment.

Some students are better suited to a larger or smaller campus in contrast to their present location. Other students want a college that is more or less academically intense and challenging, is more or less traditional, or has more opportunities in the arts, music, or sports.

Another possibility is that the discomfort you feel at school has more to do with your personal development and your ambivalence about what you want from the college experience. Sometimes students who are unhappy or unfulfilled at college are at a point in their lives where they need to do more self-reflection and introspection. Their unhappiness stems less from the college they are attending than other personal or external issues in their own lives. In those cases, it's better to stay put and keep making forward progress in your education while you take time to address these other issues or just to take a year off from college till you feel you want and are ready to return.

Many other reasons also lead students to consider transferring. Changes in one's family—through death, illness, divorce, or a job loss—may require a move to a less expensive college or one closer to home. Some students may decide they wish to live closer to their parent(s) or to a partner they see as a future spouse. Some colleges may not have adequate child care or may not be hospitable to students who work all day and need to take evening courses. Other students dislike a particular college's size (too large or too small) or environment (urban or rural). Some minority students find a particular campus climate inhospitable, and others dislike the lack of diversity.

Transferring to another college is a perfectly reasonable option, but don't act precipitously if you're thinking about transferring. It can be a good and necessary choice for you, but take your time to decide. You can apply to transfer to other colleges without dropping out of your current school. That will buy you time to see if the negative impressions and difficult circumstances persist throughout the school year.

Whatever college(s) you attend as you pursue your degree, you want to have a rewarding and fulfilling experience. Be sure changing colleges will help you achieve that goal.

<hr/>

ROBERT CHEN—*"Would You Be Willing to Write a Reference Letter for Me?"*

Robert Chen was a hardworking, good-natured student, and everyone liked him. He certainly wasn't the first person you'd notice in a group of students, because he wasn't loud or boisterous. He didn't wish to be one of the leaders among his friends or in different organizations. Robert did participate, however, and he did have many friends. He also did very well in all of his classes.

Robert was one of the quieter students in his classes, too, and he wondered whether any of his teachers noticed him. When he did speak, however, he had some interesting things to say that were worth paying attention to. He always came to class prepared, and he was a very good writer. In his larger lecture classes, it would have been difficult for any professor to notice him, but in his small seminar and discussion classes, a dedicated teacher would have easily noticed how he stood out for always being present, interested, and having good insights.

During Robert's second term, he began to look for summer jobs and internships. Most applications required him to list references, and he immediately thought of his former high school teachers and employers from home. He recognized that it wouldn't work to list high school teachers now that he was in college.

He had known that at some point he would need references from college professors, but he hadn't anticipated that that would happen till he was applying for graduate school.

Robert was aware that he had made little, if any, effort to meet his professors. He hadn't stayed after class to talk with them, and he hadn't gone to office hours except for his one teacher who made it a class requirement. Robert knew he was on the quiet side, but he felt badly that he might be penalized for that.

As the deadlines for his various applications grew near, Robert became more anxious. He felt paralyzed. Which professors could he ask? What if they said no? What if they wouldn't write a good letter on his behalf? How do you even go about asking a professor for a recommendation letter?

Robert finally decided to take a chance. He got up the courage to go to see one of his professors who had written some very complimentary comments on his paper in the previous term. To his dismay, a note on the professor's door said that he was out sick and wouldn't be in for office hours.

Robert didn't have time to wait till the professor held office hours again. He decided to send the professor an e-mail, saying that he hoped he remembered him from the last term, that he had come to office hours to ask for the reference letter, and that he hadn't been in. Robert anxiously checked his e-mail every hour to see if the professor would respond. With each passing hour, Robert grew more discouraged. "He must not remember me," Robert thought to himself.

The next morning, Robert decided to check his e-mail before he went to class. There it was. His professor had written back. The note was matter-of-fact but very kind. The professor told Robert that he would be happy to serve as a reference, that of course he remembered Robert's good class work, and that Robert should write back with details about what the professor needed to do.

Robert was so relieved. He let out a big sigh of relief and let himself relax for the first time in weeks. In fact, all Robert needed at this point was to list the name and contact information for his references. He didn't even need a letter yet.

But Robert had begun the process of making the request for references in college, and he had been successful. He was very pleased with himself for going ahead and asking, but he also felt terrific that his professor had noticed and remembered him and would be willing to take the time to write a complimentary letter on his behalf. To Robert, it felt like it had been worth all his worrying. He now felt like he was really making it in college, and it was a wonderful feeling!

99   Take a Summer Vacation

It's important that you take vacations, enjoy them, and put your academic work behind you for the time that you have off.

The culture of the United States teaches an ambivalent attitude toward vacations. You are told to study hard and work hard all year to save up for vacation time, but then when you go on vacation you are made to feel guilty for not being sufficiently workaholic. While on vacation, you will see students studying for exams and writing papers on their laptops and their parents checking in at work via their cell phone. I encourage you not to be one of these people and to fully enjoy the days you set aside for vacation.

Vacations need not be expensive. What you need is a change, a break from your everyday routine. You need to be renewed.

You will know you are renewed when you find you have new ways of looking at what had been a vexing problem prior to vacation. You will be able to put aside differences with your friends, realizing that all your angst was over a rather meaningless and trivial matter. You will come back to school with new energy and ready to take on new projects and leadership roles.

You may be surprised to find how refreshed your mind is. The book that you had so much trouble concentrating on before vacation now seems interesting and engaging. The coming semester's course load doesn't seem so daunting. The economics final that had you in a panic now seems like it didn't go as bad as you first imagined.

Vacations are not extra workdays. Take a break and enjoy yourself. It will help you be a stronger student.

100 Investigate Possible Career Choices

College is a good time to begin thinking seriously about career choices. As you explore the world of ideas, it's a time to find out about yourself, your likes and dislikes, your skills and challenges, and what kind of issues and tasks you find most stimulating. It's also a time to examine how you might fit best in the professional world of work.

It is not a good idea to think of your college education as career training. If you think of college as simply training for a profession, then you may get a good job credential from your college in the form of your diploma, but you will have missed out on a good college education. College is about learning and education. What you learn will no doubt be critical in whatever professional field you choose, but you should focus on learning as your priority.

How should you approach your career exploration? You should take a wide variety of courses to get an idea of where your interests lie. You should participate in extracurricular activities to see how you like being involved in organizations and what activities hold your interest.

You should do an internship or get a job in a field that carries some initial interest for you.

As you get more serious and focused about your studies, go to the career center or your department to find out how your academic interests line up and prepare you for different kinds of careers. You'll be surprised at how expansive your opportunities are regardless of your field of study. Every professional position will require you to be able to think critically, broadly, and innovatively. You will be called upon to do a wide range of tasks and to use a variety of skills in almost any field you choose. You may change careers more than once or twice, and you will certainly be required to retool and reconceptualize your work even in the unlikely event that you stay in the same career over a lifetime.

As you pursue a major, you will want to begin considering the opportunity to attend graduate and professional schools. You also may decide to go directly into the workforce. Be sure to keep all of your options open. While you may feel today that you can't conceive of attending school beyond your undergraduate degree, you may feel very differently as you enter your senior year of college. Similarly, going directly into the workforce after college is by no means an indication that you won't be entering a graduate program within a few years.

Those students who enter college with clear preprofessional goals, like business, law, medicine, and especially engineering, will have a much more defined curriculum right from the first year of college. While that training is important for your professional preparation, be careful to hold onto as much of the unique opportunity of a liberal arts education as you can. Take full advantage of your elective courses. Don't miss out on an undergraduate education because you are in such a hurry to advance professionally. You'll be working in that profession for the next forty or fifty years; your college education comes only once and for just a very few years in your lifetime.

A college education is essential for professional careers today. Do take advantage of your education to begin thinking about and preparing for your professional life. At the same time, don't be so focused on what's ahead that you don't allow yourself to fully experience and enjoy today the gift that a college education represents. You will find that your broad, liberal arts education will serve you well throughout your life and in every aspect of your career.

101 Remember Your College Accomplishments

You will have numerous accomplishments, large and small, during your college years. Be sure to make a note of them in a journal, in a file, or on your résumé so that you can fondly remember these special moments and highlights of your college years. Time will go by so quickly that unless you have an intentional, organized system for keeping memories, you will lose track of so much good that you have done.

Some of your accomplishments will be in the academic arena. You may get comments from a professor expressing what an outstanding exam or paper you've written. Keep that paper and hold onto those special words. You may be more formally recognized by being placed on the college honor roll or acknowledged at a college honors ceremony. You might be invited to serve on a university policy committee or to give input into departmental curricular projects. You may win a prize for poetry, participate on the debate team, star in a theatrical performance, exhibit artwork, or be invited to attend a conference to talk about your research.

Other accomplishments will be based on your personal and community achievements. You might experience a new friendship or a first kiss—jot a note down about the experience. You may win a scholarship for civic involvement, be elected or appointed to a leadership position in an organization, or get a promotion at your workplace. You might play in the school's marching band, make the varsity gymnastics team, or score the winning goal in an intramural game. Keep a file of all these accomplishments. Someone you admire may say something very complimentary about you—write in a journal how you felt.

If you're not the kind of person who keeps good files, then make sure you make good mental images of your accomplishments. First of all, be sure you accept the recognition you receive. You don't need to feel you're gloating to feel good about yourself. Try to hold onto the image of a compliment from someone you respect, a fun day with a good friend, or praise from one of your professors.

When you begin college, it will seem like you have an endless road ahead of you. You will soon find that your college days will go by very quickly. Hold onto your best memories, even as you continue to create special, new ones each and every day.

Text design by Jillian Downey
Typesetting by Huron Valley Graphics, Ann Arbor, Michigan
Text font: New Baskerville
Display font: Scala Sans

"British printer John Baskerville of Birmingham created the types that bear his name in about 1752. George Jones designed this version of Baskerville for Linotype-Hell in 1930, and the International Typeface Corporation licensed it in 1982."

—Courtesy www.adobe.com

Scala Sans was designed by Martin Majoor in 1990 and published by www.FontFont.com.

—Courtesy www.identifont.com